Council of Europe Publishing

Cover design: Graphic Design Workshop, Council of Europe

Council of Europe Publishing
F-67075 Strasbourg Cedex

ISBN 92-871-3874-5
© Council of Europe, May 1999
Printed in Germany

Contents

ACKNOWLEDGEMENTS

The authors would like to thank the following persons for their help and support in the preparation of this volume:

Laryssa Denysenko, Anne Ferrazzini, Bosse Hedberg, Tanja Kleinsorge, Konstantyn Mazur, members of the Committee on Legal Affairs and Human Rights.

This collection was edited by Tanja Kleinsorge and Barbara Zatlokal.

PREFACE

In 1998, for the first time in European history, none of the then forty member states of the Council of Europe carried out capital punishment. Death sentences were pronounced in several countries; in ten of them capital punishment remains on the statute book. But even these ten states respected moratoria they had established, either *de jure* or *de facto*. The only exception to this rule was noted in Chechnya, a region where the central authorities of the Russian Federation were not able to exercise administrative control.

Will 1998 stand out as an exceptional *annus mirabilis*, or was it the precursor of a lasting enlightened era in European penal practice? Only the future can tell. But what we can tell already now – and what is indeed expressed eloquently in this book – is that the abolitionist cause has taken giant strides forward in recent years. Indeed, it is difficult to imagine that this trend, as demonstrated by political and legal developments, could be reversed. However, vigilance and sustained efforts remain necessary.

The Protocol No. 6 to the European Convention on Human Rights, adopted in 1983, has to date been ratified by thirty member states of the Council of Europe, and in recent years no country has been admitted into the Organisation without having either abolished the death penalty or promised to do so in the near future, with a commitment to uphold a strict moratorium in the meantime. The Parliamentary Assembly is vigorously seeking to ensure that such pledges are honoured, as evident, among other things, from its latest recommendation based on the Wohlwend Report adopted by the Assembly's Standing Committee.

The present volume demonstrates how a number of separate initiatives have contributed to humanising legislation in one country after another. If ever one were justified to speak of "virtuous circles", this is certainly such a case; clearly good examples and peer pressure have played a very important role in convincing governments and legislators alike that the death penalty belongs to a primitive and uncivilised past. It is, of course, a form of punishment still largely supported by public opinion in some countries, and this resistance is still strongly felt in certain parliaments. But is the role of legislators simply to reflect public opinion, or is it also to lead? For those parliamentarians still wrestling with this question, the chapter by the Deputy Secretary General, Hans Christian Krüger, contains a sobering thought. The revenge instinct may indeed be a very strong human propensity, but human instincts are not necessarily the best guideline for enlightened legislation. The purpose of law is not to imitate nature but, wherever needed, to correct it.

At the second summit of the Council of Europe in 1997, the heads of state and government called, in no uncertain terms, for the abolition of capital punishment. This book bears out why capital punishment has no place in a civilised society.

Daniel Tarschys
Secretary General of the Council of Europe

INTRODUCTION – THE IMPORTANCE OF ABOLISHING THE DEATH PENALTY

Roger Hood, Director, Centre for Criminological Research, University of Oxford and Fellow, All Souls' College, Oxford

---

These essays celebrate the virtual abandonment of the death penalty from the statute books of European countries and a moratorium on executions in all member states of the Council of Europe who have yet to abolish the death penalty in law. Indeed, there is a virtual cessation of executions right across the continent. Yet the authors do not ignore the fact that in some countries this has been achieved against the grain of strong public and political sentiment in favour of capital punishment. Thus, there is still a need to reinforce the case for abolition in these countries as well as to persuade retentionist states outside Europe that the death penalty can no longer be justified.

It is always worth restating what the main objections are to capital punishment being used as an instrument of state punishment. They are so well known, of course, that a brief summary will suffice:

- The death penalty is an extreme example of torture, a form of punishment that violates human rights. It is therefore an illegitimate mode of punishment for a state to employ.

- There is no convincing evidence that the rate of murder (or any other crime threatened with the death penalty) is consistently lower when the death penalty is on the statute book and enforced by executions. When all the circumstances surrounding the way in which capital punishment is used in democratic states and under the rule of law are taken into account, it has not proved to be a more effective deterrent than the alternative sanctions of life or long-term imprisonment.

- In countries which abide by the rule of law and take into account mitigating as well as aggravating circumstances, capital punishment is, in practice, inflicted only in a relatively small proportion of the cases which could legally fall within its scope. Experience has shown that it cannot be administered without an unacceptable degree of arbitrariness, inequity and discrimination even when it is retained only for a restricted category of murders.

- It is counterproductive in the moral message it conveys, for it legitimises the very behaviour – killing – which the law seeks to repress. This is especially true when those executed appear as scapegoats and excite pity, and even more so when occasionally the innocent are executed – an inevitable consequence of capital punishment. It therefore undermines the legitimacy and moral authority of the whole legal system.

Europe in the abolitionist vanguard

While the first attempts by enlightened European rulers at the end of the eighteenth century to abolish capital punishment were soon reversed, the movement to restrict it to murder was successful in many countries by the mid-nineteenth century. In the 1850s the mid-American states of Michigan and Wisconsin abolished the death penalty completely for murder, and Venezuela became the first country to abolish it for all crimes in 1863. Portugal (where there had been no executions since 1843), the first European country to abolish capital punishment for murder in 1867, was soon followed by the Netherlands, Romania, Italy, and Norway. After the first world war they were joined by Sweden, Denmark and Switzerland. With the end of fascist tyranny capital punishment was abandoned first by Italy in 1944 (it had been restored by Mussolini) and then by the Federal Republic of Germany in 1949. Thus, by the time that Marc Ancel made his survey for the Council of Europe in 1962 executions were being carried out in western Europe – usually quite rarely – only in the United Kingdom, France, Greece, the Irish Republic, Spain and Turkey. It was on the statute book, as Philippe Toussaint points out, but unused in Belgium and Luxembourg. All of these countries with the exception of Turkey, soon abandoned capital punishment, the last execution taking place in France in 1977, over twenty years ago. Turkey has not executed anyone since 1984.

Capital punishment had been, of course, endemic in all the countries of eastern Europe which formed the former "Soviet bloc", although in some countries, as Robert Fico reveals in relation to Czechoslovakia, it was used more as a tool for political suppression than for ordinary offenders. Yet, once free of Soviet domination and totalitarian government they quickly began to rid themselves entirely of capital punishment. The movement began with the former German Democratic Republic in 1987, gathered pace after the fall of Ceauşescu in Romania in 1989, spread quickly to Hungary and the former Czechoslovakia in 1990 and then to many other former communist states.

Yet what marks out the modern period from the past, when abolition was very much an internal "national" matter, is the development of a trans-European political movement to make abolition of the death penalty the touchstone of acceptable national standards of respect for human rights. As Hans Christian Krüger points out, it was towards the end of the 1970s that the Committee of Ministers of the Council of Europe first began to consider the question of capital punishment as a human rights issue. And Eric Prokosch reminds us that it is less than twenty years ago that Protocol No. 6 to the European Convention on Human Rights (ECHR), calling for the abolition of the death penalty in peacetime, was opened for signature. Some countries, as Caroline Ravaud and Stephan Treschel recall, were slower than others to ratify the protocol. Indeed the United Kingdom signed the Protocol only in January of 1999 after the last antiquated vestiges of the death penalty (other than in military law) were abolished on the initiative of backbench MPs, some thirty years after it had been abolished for murder. At the time of writing twenty-eight states have ratified the protocol, seven more (Albania, Lithuania, Bulgaria, Russia, Latvia, Ukraine and the United Kingdom) have signed it. Turkey remains the only member of the Council of Europe to have done neither.

The most important political decision came in the wake of the first summit of the Council of Europe held in Vienna in 1993, which laid down that applicant states should, among other things, undertake to sign and ratify the European Convention on Human Rights. Five years ago, following the influential report in 1994 by Hans Göran Franck on The Abolition of the Death Penalty, the Parliamentary Assembly made it a condition that any country which wished to become a member of the Council of Europe should agree to implement an immediate moratorium on executions and then sign and ratify, within a set number of years, Protocol No. 6 to the ECHR. We are told that the aspiration to be accepted as part of the European political community had a decisive influence on the decision of Czechoslovakia to get rid of the death penalty. And, as Renate Wohlwend, Anatoly Pristavkin and Serhiy Holovatiy so vividly recount, the desire to be a member of the Council of Europe has proved to be a potent factor in persuading Russia and Ukraine – despite their initial serious breaches of their obligations to honour the moratorium – now to refrain from further executions.

Recently, the European Union similarly made the abolition of capital punishment a pre-condition for membership and in 1998 it embarked on a diplomatic policy to persuade other nations through the adoption of Guidelines to European Union Policy towards Third Countries on the Death Penalty. These stressed that "the death penalty has no place in the penal systems of modern civilised societies" and "abolition of the death penalty contributes to the enhancement of human dignity and the progressive development of human rights". Indeed as Roberto Toscano emphasises, the European stance is not to accept the argument that capital punishment can be defined in "relativistic" religious or cultural terms or as a matter purely for national sovereignty. Rather it has become transformed into an issue of an international "human rights norm". This is reflected in what Caroline Ravaud and Stephen Treschel call a "kind of moral consensus" among member states of the Council of Europe – that persons shall not be extradited to countries with the death penalty unless there are strong guarantees that it will not be enforced.

The speed of change in European attitudes can be gauged from reading the excellent report to the Council of Europe in 1962 on The Death Penalty in European Countries presented by the distinguished French jurist Marc Ancel. Following Beccaria, he remarked that "even the most convinced abolitionists realise that there may be special circumstances, or particularly troublous times, which justify the introduction of the death penalty for a limited period". Yet such has been the momentum that, just over thirty years later, the majority of European countries has abolished capital punishment absolutely. Indeed a proposal is on the table for a further protocol banning capital punishment in war as well as in peacetime.

The situation of the new abolitionist states

The writers from the "new abolitionist" countries of eastern Europe raise some difficult issues. They all show that the abolitionist cause is made fragile by an atmosphere of social insecurity, particularly when a spate of horrifying crimes produces a wave of public revulsion and anger. Such events, as Michel Forst stresses, delayed abolition of the death penalty in France. Robert Fico, Serhiy Holovatiy and Anatoly Pristavkin all describe how the economic and political transformation of their countries have been accompanied by a rise in crime which has stimulated a popular clamour to maintain a strong deterrent. In many of these countries, abolition has not – as it was in most western European states – been a gradual process, that is following a period in which capital punishment had been very rarely used. The former Soviet Union had an execution rate per head of population seven times higher than the United States as a whole, even including abolitionist and non-executing states. Abolition of the death penalty in this context can all too easily be interpreted by politicians as a sign of the further weakening of the fabric of social order. This has led Caroline Ravaud and Stefan Treschel to question the political sensitivity of demanding so much so soon from these countries. Indeed Robert Fico warns of the danger of a rift opening up between the official policy of the state and public demand for better protection against the growing threat of crime, of which murder is always a potent symbol.

A further problem relates to finding an acceptable alternative to capital punishment. For example, as Renate Wohlwend relates, prison conditions in the Ukraine do not appear to meet basic human rights standards. In Russia, according to Anatoly Pristavkin, conditions of confinement are said to be so bad that prisoners are writing to the Russian Presidential Pardons Commission begging to be executed so as to be put out of their misery. It cannot be right to replace one abuse of human rights by another.

What can be said that would be helpful to abolitionists in such situations? First, that they should recognise that the evidence relating to deterrence, most of it coming from North America, is complex. It should not be over-simplified by inapt comparisons. For example, the argument that abolition was followed by a decline in the murder rate in Canada is unlikely to prove an effective weapon in the debate when the murder rate is clearly rising. The lesson from the deterrence literature is not that abolition is inevitably followed by a decline in murder, but that there is no causal connection between the use of capital punishment and the murder rate. The rise and fall of murder rates are influenced by a complexity of demographic and social factors, including the effectiveness of police in bringing perpetrators to justice, rather than the distant threat of execution.

Secondly, it is precisely when there are strong reactions to serious crimes that the use of the death penalty as an instrument of crime control is most dangerous. Pressure on the police and prosecutors to bring offenders to justice, especially those suspected of committing outrages, is likely to lead to short cuts, breaches of procedural protections, and simple myopia in investigation once a suspect is identified. One only has to think of what the consequences would have been had the United Kingdom still had the death penalty on its statute books for the crimes of which alleged IRA bombers were initially convicted. So many of those convicted of former capital crimes were subsequently found to have been wrongfully convicted on the basis of tainted evidence. In this regard, Anatoly Pristavkin's statement that prominent jurists in Russia estimate that wrongful convictions amount to between 10% and 15% of those sentenced to death is especially worrying.

Thirdly, as Robert Fico points out, these states will need to do their utmost to educate their citizens about the death penalty. Indeed, in this respect Peter Hodgkinson's contribution is a reminder that the concerns of deceased crime victims' families will need to be taken into account. Otherwise, the gulf between states and their populations may become ever wider, with potentially serious effects on the ability of governments to maintain the abolitionist position.

Fourthly, those states which abolish the death penalty in order to meet their international obligations for the protection of human rights must also meet their obligations to set up an humane and effective system of long-term imprisonment. It is only right that they should receive some aid, both expert and financial, to make this possible.

Europe in the international context

European countries can congratulate themselves for banishing a barbaric punishment from their own soil and for using their political influence to get rid of it in countries which wish to be associated with the European community of nations. Nevertheless, much needs to be done if third countries, some of whom proclaim the need for capital punishment with vigour, are to be influenced in the same direction.

There are, however, positive signs that more countries are willing to accept that capital punishment is incompatible with a political culture based on human rights. For example, who, a decade ago, would have predicted the abandonment of capital punishment in South Africa? But, of course, where religion, as in Islamic law, demands the death penalty persuasion is particularly controversial. Nevertheless, with some notable exceptions, a substantial number of countries which have the death penalty in law rarely carry out executions. They appear to recognise that, in practice, death is too harsh a penalty for many murders and that discrimination, error and other human rights issues cannot be avoided if capital punishment is regularly enforced. In other words, many retentionist countries, including India, Japan and Thailand, hang on to this penalty with apparently little commitment to use it as a vigorous means of crime control. Having forgone that justification, they will inevitably become more open to moral arguments. In this respect China is the exception, being responsible for about 80% of the executions known worldwide. Yet China has recently willingly discussed the issue with the European Union in the context of human rights and law reform.

However, the European initiative will prove difficult for as long as the United States, which defines itself as the archetypal liberal democracy and guardian of human rights, retains the death penalty. While the United States continues to reject human rights arguments on the death penalty as defined by international consensus or treaty unless they are endorsed by its own Supreme Court, appeals to other countries less wedded to these ideals will continue to have their force severely diluted. Those Caribbean countries that strongly support capital punishment are no doubt strengthened in their resolve by the policy of their powerful neighbour. The challenge for Europe is to find a way to persuade the United States, with which it shares so many values and beliefs, that the European view of the death penalty is both morally right and free from social danger.

Can Europe do anything to influence American political and judicial opinion? The demand for capital punishment in the United States is often said to rest on the popular belief that it is an essential defence against, and an appropriate reaction to, what has undoubtedly been a high rate of homicide. That rate has been falling, not it seems due to the use of executions, but to a considerable extent to changes in the demographic structure of the population. Moreover, those executed still account for only a tiny fraction of all homicides. They are more like scapegoats, killed often more than a decade after the crime occurred, rather than objects of impartial and humane justice. More to the point is the political context. Officers of justice – police, prosecutors, some judges, and the state governors with the power of clemency – are all subject to the popular vote and apparently fear to voice their opposition to capital punishment. The European experience, as chronicled in several of these essays, shows the importance of political leadership in the face of public opinion: the names of Christian Broda, Robert Badinter and François Mitterrand stand out, as does the political influence of Italy at the United Nations, eloquently described by Roberto Toscano. Those political leaders who have the courage to lead the fight against the death penalty in the United States will need to be sought out and given international recognition if they are to withstand such populist pressures.

It needs to be more generally recognised that capital punishment in the United States is, in practice, a local matter arising from crimes committed against state rather than federal law. Indeed, the federal authorities have executed no one since capital punishment was again made lawful, after the moratorium, by the Supreme Court in 1976. But state governments seem isolated from, indifferent to, and apparently ignorant of international norms relating to the application of the death penalty. There have been many proven violations of the United Nations Safeguards Guaranteeing Protection of the Rights of Those Facing the Death Penalty.[1] Further dialogue needs to be opened up with state governments, although the situation will remain difficult while the federal government refuses to withdraw its reservation to Article 6 of the International Covenant on Civil and Political Rights, which

---

1. Reproduced in Hood, R. (1996) *The Death Penalty. A Worldwide Perspective*. Second revised and up-dated edition, pp. 250-251.

prohibits the execution of anyone whose crimes were committed when they were below the age of eighteen.

Capital punishment remains in the United States, and in far too many other countries, as a cruel penal symbol comparatively rarely enforced, applied in an unacceptably arbitrary way, often in flagrant violation of international standards for the protection of prisoners, and for no demonstrable gain in the diminution of murder. Only when politicians in state and federal governments reject populism as a basis for deciding this issue will the United States and other democratic countries which retain the death penalty join those European nations who have declared that the death penalty is incompatible with a political culture which values human rights.

1. THE DEATH PENALTY VERSUS HUMAN RIGHTS

Eric Prokosch, Theme Research Co-ordinator, Amnesty International

---

Fifty years after the adoption of the United Nations' Universal Declaration of Human Rights, the trend towards worldwide abolition of the death penalty is unmistakable. When the Declaration was adopted in 1948, eight countries had abolished the death penalty for all crimes; as of November 1998, the number stands at sixty-three. More than half the countries in the world have abolished the death penalty in law or practice, and the number continues to increase.

In Europe the trend is especially remarkable: the Parliamentary Assembly of the Council of Europe now requires a commitment to abolition as a condition of entry into the organisation, and the European Union has adopted a far-reaching policy governing the promotion of abolition in non-member states. Within the United Nations, the Commission on Human Rights has called on states that still maintain the punishment "to establish a moratorium on executions, with a view to completely abolishing the death penalty" (Resolution 1998/8 of 3 April 1998). Yet there are still calls for the use or extension of the death penalty, often in response to public concern about crime.

What do these matters have to do with human rights?

Understanding the death penalty as a human rights violation

Amnesty International opposes the death penalty as a violation of fundamental human rights – the right to life and the right not to be subjected to cruel, inhuman or degrading treatment or punishment. Both of these rights are recognised in the Universal Declaration of Human Rights, other international and regional human rights instruments and national constitutions and laws.

Defence of life and defence of the state may be held to justify, in some cases, the taking of life by state officials; for example, when law-enforcement officials must act immediately to save their own lives or those of others or when a country is engaged in armed conflict. Even in such situations the use of lethal force is surrounded by internationally accepted standards of human rights and humanitarian law to inhibit abuse.

The death penalty, however, is not an act of defence against an immediate threat to life. It is the premeditated killing of a prisoner for the purpose of punishment – a purpose which can be met by other means.

The cruelty of torture is evident. Like torture, an execution constitutes an extreme physical and mental assault on a person already rendered helpless by government authorities. The cruelty of the death penalty is manifest not only in the execution but in the time spent under sentence of death, during which the prisoner is constantly contemplating his or her own death at the hands of the state. This cruelty cannot be justified, no matter how cruel the crime of which the prisoner has been convicted.

If it is impermissible to cause grievous physical and mental harm to a prisoner by subjecting him or her to electric shocks and mock executions, how can it be permissible for public officials to attack not only the body or the mind, but the prisoner's very life?

Threatening to kill a prisoner can be one of the most fearsome forms of torture. As torture, it is prohibited. How can it be permissible to subject a prisoner to the same threat in the form of a death sentence, passed by a court of law and due to be carried out by the prison authorities?

The cruelty of the death penalty extends beyond the prisoner to the prisoner's family, to the prison guards and to the officials who have to carry out an execution. Information from various parts of the world shows that the role of an executioner can be deeply disturbing, even traumatic. Judges, prosecutors and other officials may also experience difficult moral dilemmas if the roles they are required to play in administering the death penalty conflict with their own ethical views.

The right to life and the right not to be subjected to cruel, inhuman or degrading treatment or punishment are the two human rights most often cited in debates about the death penalty. But the death penalty also attacks other rights.

As indicated by the annual reports of the United Nations Commission on Human Rights by its Special Rapporteur on Extrajudicial, Summary or Arbitrary Executions and by Amnesty International's own information, in many cases prisoners are sentenced to death in trials which do not conform to international norms for a fair trial. Prisoners facing a possible death sentence are often represented by inexperienced lawyers, and sometimes by no lawyer at all. The defendants may not understand the charges or the evidence against them, especially if they are not conversant with the language used in court. Facilities for interpretation and translation of court documents are often inadequate. In some cases prisoners are unable to exercise their right to appeal to a court of higher jurisdiction and the right to petition for clemency or commutation of the death sentence. In some jurisdictions, capital cases are heard before special or military courts using summary procedures. Such practices undermine the right to a fair trial and are in violation of standards recognised in international human rights instruments.

The death penalty is often used disproportionately against members of disadvantaged social groups, and thus in a discriminatory fashion, contrary to Articles 2 and 7 of the Universal Declaration of Human Rights. It is the ultimate denial of the dignity and worth of the human person, affirmed in the preamble to the Universal Declaration of Human Rights.

There is no criminological justification for the death penalty which would outweigh the human rights grounds for abolishing it. The argument that the death penalty is needed to deter crime has become discredited by the consistent lack of scientific evidence that it does so more effectively than other punishments. The death penalty negates the internationally accepted penological goal of rehabilitating the offender.

Restriction through international standards

International human rights standards have developed in a way that favours ever tighter restrictions on the scope of the death penalty. This progressive narrowing of the death penalty is mirrored by actual practice in most states which still use the punishment.

Progressive restriction as a goal

In a resolution on capital punishment, the United Nations General Assembly in 1971 affirmed that "in order fully to guarantee the right to life, provided for in Article 3 of the Universal Declaration of Human Rights, the main objective to be pursued is that of progressively restricting the number of offences for which capital punishment may be imposed, with a view to the desirability of abolishing this punishment in all countries" (Resolution 2857 (XXVI) of 20 December 1971). The goal of progressive restriction of capital offences was reiterated by the General Assembly in 1977 (Resolution 32/61 of 8 December 1977), by the United Nations Commission on Human Rights in Resolutions 1997/12 of 3 April 1997 and Resolution 1998/8 of 3 April 1998, and by the European Union in the Guidelines to European Union Policy towards Third Countries on the Death Penalty (EU Guidelines), adopted in 1998.

Restriction to the most serious offences

The International Covenant on Civil and Political Rights (ICCPR), adopted by the United Nations General Assembly in 1966, states in Article 6 (2): "In countries which have not abolished the death penalty, sentence of death may be imposed only for the most serious crimes...".

In a general comment on Article 6 of the ICCPR, the Human Rights Committee established under that treaty stated that "the expression 'most serious crimes' must be read restrictively to mean that the death penalty should be a quite exceptional measure" (general comment 6, adopted by the Committee at its 16th Session on 27 July 1982).

The United Nations Economic and Social Council, in the Safeguards Guaranteeing Protection of the Rights of Those Facing the Death Penalty, adopted in 1984 (ECOSOC Safeguards), reiterated that the death penalty should be imposed only for the most serious crimes and stated that the scope of these crimes "should not go beyond intentional crimes with lethal or other extremely grave consequences".

There have been various specific standards and statements about the crimes for which the death penalty should not be used. Article 4(4) of the American Convention on Human Rights (ACHR) states that the death penalty shall not be inflicted "for political offences or related common crimes". The Human Rights Committee has stated that "the imposition ... of the death penalty for offences which cannot be characterised as the most serious, including apostasy, committing a third homosexual act, illicit sex, embezzlement by officials, and theft by force, is incompatible with Article 6 of the Covenant" (United Nations Document No. CCPR/C/79/Add.5, paragraph 8). The United Nations Special Rapporteur on Extrajudicial, Summary or Arbitrary Executions has stated that the death penalty "should be eliminated for crimes such as economic crimes and drug-related offences" (United Nations Document No. E/CN.4/1997/60, 24 December 1996, paragraph 91).

The international standard of restricting the death penalty to the most serious crimes, in particular to those with lethal consequences, is broadly reflected in practice. Most states which continue to carry out executions today do so only for murder, although they may retain the death penalty in law for other crimes. Moreover, the rate of executions in most such countries has declined to a point where it represents only a tiny fraction in relation to the number of reported murders. (The most outstanding exception is China, which carries out more executions than all other countries combined, and continues to execute prisoners for non-violent offences including theft and embezzlement.)

A further development in the restriction of capital offences is the adoption by an international conference in Rome in July 1998 of the Statute of the International Criminal Court, in which the death penalty is not provided for what are arguably the most heinous crimes of all – genocide, other crimes against humanity and war crimes. Similarly, the United Nations Security Council excluded the death penalty for these grave crimes in 1993 and 1994 when it established the International Criminal Tribunals for the former Yugoslavia and for Rwanda. If these decisions are read together with the well-established standard that the death penalty should be used only for the most serious crimes in countries which have not abolished it, the implication is that the death penalty should not be used at all. If the use of the death penalty is excluded for the most serious international crimes, it can hardly be countenanced for lesser crimes.

Restriction of applicable offenders

International standards have also developed in such a way as to exclude more and more categories of people from those against whom the death penalty might be used in countries which have not abolished it.

- The exclusion of juvenile offenders, that is those under 18 years old at the time of the offence, is so widely accepted in law and practice that it is approaching the status of a norm of customary international law. The prohibition on sentencing juvenile offenders to death has been set out in the ICCPR (Article 6(5)), the ACHR (Article 4(5)), the ECOSOC Safeguards, the 4th Geneva Convention of 1949 relative to the Protection of Civilian Persons in Time of War and the two Additional Protocols of 1977 to the Geneva Conventions of 1949 and, more recently, in the Convention on the Rights of the Child (Article 37(a)), which has been ratified by all but two United Nations member states. The prohibition is widely observed in practice. Between January 1990 and October 1998 Amnesty International documented only eighteen executions of juvenile offenders worldwide, carried out in six countries. Half of the executions were carried out in just one country, the United States of America.

- The exclusion of pregnant women, new mothers, and people over 70 years of age, set out variously in the ICCPR, the ACHR and the ECOSOC Safeguards, are also widely observed in practice.

- The ECOSOC Safeguards also state that executions shall not be carried out on "persons who have become *insane*" (emphasis added), and in Resolution 1989/64, adopted on 24 May 1989, ECOSOC recommended that United Nations member states eliminate the death penalty "for persons suffering from *mental retardation* or extremely limited mental competence, whether at the stage of sentence or execution" (emphasis added). These exclusions are less widely observed. Amnesty International has documented many cases of prisoners sentenced to death and – sometimes – executed, particularly in the United States, who were of extremely limited mental ability.

Procedural safeguards

Procedural safeguards to be followed in all death penalty cases have been set out in Article 6 of the ICCPR and Article 4 of the ACHR and reiterated and elaborated upon in the ECOSOC Safeguards and other United Nations' resolutions. They include all international norms for a fair trial, including the right to appeal to a higher court, and the right to petition for clemency. In General Assembly Resolution 2393 (XXIII) of 26 November 1968 and successive resolutions, the United Nations has repeatedly stated its wish to ensure the most careful legal procedures and the greatest possible safeguards for those accused in capital cases in countries where the death penalty has not been abolished. The need to respect minimum standards in death penalty cases is also reflected in the EU Guidelines.

Although the safeguards exist in principle in many countries which retain the death penalty, they are often not fully observed in practice, and even where an effort is made to observe them, the use of the death penalty often remains arbitrary. Factors such as inadequate legal aid and prosecutorial discretion result in some defendants being sentenced to death and executed while others convicted of similar crimes are not. The safeguards have failed to prevent the arbitrary use of the death penalty or to preclude its use against people innocent of the crimes of which they were convicted.

The emergence of abolition as a human rights norm

International bodies have increasingly made statements and adopted policies favouring abolition on human rights grounds. These statements and policies are beginning to be backed up by national court decisions ruling out the death penalty as a violation of human rights.

Statements and policies

In Resolution 2857 (XXVI) of 20 December 1971, cited above, the United Nations General Assembly affirmed the desirability of abolishing the death penalty in all countries. The desirability of abolishing the death penalty was reiterated in General Assembly Resolution 32/61 of 8 December 1977 and – most recently – by the United Nations Commission on Human Rights in Resolution 1998/8 of 3 April 1998.

In its general comment on Article 6 of the ICCPR, cited above, the Human Rights Committee stated that Article 6 "refers generally to abolition [of the death penalty] in terms which strongly suggest ... that abolition is desirable. The Committee concludes that all measures of abolition should be considered as progress in the enjoyment of the right to life...

In Resolution 1997/12 of 3 April 1997, the United Nations Commission on Human Rights expressed its conviction "that abolition of the death penalty contributes to the enhancement of human dignity and to the progressive development of human rights". This statement was reiterated by the Commission on Human Rights in Resolution 1998/8 of 3 April 1998.

The United Nations Special Rapporteur on Extrajudicial, Summary or Arbitrary Executions has stated that he "strongly supports the conclusions of the Human Rights Committee and emphasises that the abolition of capital punishment is most desirable in order fully to respect the right to life" (United Nations Document No. E/CN.4/1997/60, paragraph 79). He has urged governments of countries where the death penalty is still enforced "to deploy every effort that could lead to its abolition" (United Nations Document No. A/51/457, paragraph 145).

In Resolution 727 of 22 April 1980, the Parliamentary Assembly of the Council of Europe stated that "capital punishment is inhuman" and appealed to the parliaments of member states which retained the death penalty for peacetime offences to abolish it. It widened the appeal in Resolution 1044 (1994) of 4 October 1994, calling "upon all the parliaments in the world which have not yet abolished the death penalty, to do so promptly following the example of the majority of Council of Europe member states". It stated that it "considers that the death penalty has no legitimate place in the penal systems of modern civilised societies, and that its application may well be compared with torture and be seen as inhuman and degrading punishment within the meaning of Article 3 of the European Convention on Human Rights" (Recommendation 1246 (1994)).

The EU Guidelines, cited above, state that "abolition of the death penalty contributes to the enhancement of human dignity and the progressive development of human rights". The Guidelines establish as a European Union objective "to work towards universal abolition of the death penalty as a strongly held policy view agreed by all EU member states".

National court decisions

On 24 October 1990 the Hungarian Constitutional Court declared that the death penalty violates the "inherent right to life and human dignity" as provided under Article 54 of the country's constitution. The judgment had the effect of abolishing the death penalty for all crimes in Hungary.

On 6 June 1995 the South African Constitutional Court declared the death penalty to be incompatible with the prohibition of "cruel, inhuman or degrading treatment or punishment" under the country's interim constitution.[1] Eight of the eleven judges also found that the death penalty violates the right to life. The judgment had the effect of abolishing the death penalty for murder.

International abolitionist treaties

The community of nations has adopted three international treaties providing for the abolition of the death penalty; one is of worldwide scope, the other two are regional. In order of adoption, they are Protocol No. 6 to the Convention for the Protection of Human Rights and Fundamental Freedoms (European Convention on Human Rights) concerning the abolition of the death penalty, adopted by the Council of Europe in 1982; the Second Optional Protocol to the International Covenant on Civil and Political Rights, aiming at the abolition of the death penalty, adopted by the United Nations General Assembly in 1989; and the Protocol to the American Convention on Human Rights to Abolish the Death Penalty, adopted by the General Assembly of the Organisation of American States in 1990. Protocol No. 6 to the European Convention on Human Rights provides for the abolition of the death penalty in peacetime; the other two treaties provide for the total abolition of the death penalty but allow states parties to retain the death penalty in time of war if they make a declaration to that effect at the time of ratification or accession.

---

1. *Makwanyane and Mcbunu v. The State* (1995), *Human Rights Law Journal* Vol. 16, pp. 154-208 paragraphs 95, 146.

Protocol No. 6 is the most widely ratified of the three in comparison to the number of states parties to the parent treaty; as of October 1998 it had been ratified by twenty-eight states and signed by another five. The Second Optional Protocol to the ICCPR had been ratified by thirty-three states as of the same date and signed by another three, while the Protocol to the American Convention on Human Rights to Abolish the Death Penalty had been ratified by six states and signed by one other. The numbers of signatories and states parties continue to grow. In 1998 alone Estonia ratified and Latvia signed Protocol No. 6, Nepal ratified the Second Optional Protocol to the ICCPR and Costa Rica and Ecuador ratified the American protocol.

The road to abolition

The pace of abolition has accelerated in the second half of the twentieth century, and especially in the past twenty years. At the beginning of the century, only three states had permanently abolished the death penalty for all crimes: Costa Rica, San Marino and Venezuela. In 1948, the number stood at eight. By the end of 1978 it had risen to nineteen. During the past twenty years the number has more than tripled.

Sixty-three countries today have abolished the death penalty for all crimes. Another sixteen countries have abolished the death penalty for all but exceptional crimes such as wartime crimes.

Alongside the countries which have abolished the death penalty for all crimes or for ordinary crimes only, there are twenty-four which can be considered abolitionist *de facto*, in that they retain the death penalty in law but have not carried out any executions for the past ten years, or have made an international commitment not to do so. As Roger Hood has stated,[1] the death penalty in these countries "has a far greater symbolic than practical significance".

These figures make for a total of 103 countries which have abolished the death penalty in law or practice. Ninety-two other countries could be said to retain the death penalty, but the number of countries which actually execute prisoners in any one year is much smaller. In 1997, for example, Amnesty International recorded 2 607 executions in forty countries worldwide. The vast majority of reported executions, 85%, were carried out in just four countries: China, Iran, Saudi Arabia and the United States of America.

---

1. Hood R. (1996), ibid, p. 79.

As indicated above, these developments in law and practice nationally have been mirrored by the development of international standards restricting the application of the death penalty and affirming the desirability of abolition on human rights grounds. As William A. Schabas has observed,[3] "Given the enormous and rapid progress in the development of international norms respecting the death penalty since the end of the second world war, the general acceptance of abolition and its elevation to a customary norm of international law, perhaps even a norm of *jus cogens*, may be envisaged in the not too distant future".

The trend to abolition seems inexorable, yet the battle has to be fought over and over again. Each country has to go through a process which is often long and painful, examining for itself the arguments for and against, before finally, we hope, rejecting the death penalty.

Even after abolition, there may be calls to bring the death penalty back. If the calls are serious enough, the arguments have to be gone through again.

The decision to abolish the death penalty has to be taken by the government and the legislators. This decision can be taken even though the majority of the public favour the death penalty. Historically, this has probably almost always been the case. Yet when the death penalty is abolished, usually there is no great public outcry, and once abolished, it almost always stays abolished.

This must mean that although the majority of the public in a given country favours the death penalty, it is also the case that a majority of the public is willing to accept abolition. This is a feature of public opinion which is not usually revealed by polls asking respondents to state their position on the death penalty. If the questions were more sophisticated, the polls would probably give a better sense of the complexities of public opinion and the extent to which it is based on an accurate understanding of the actual situation of criminality in the country, its causes and the means available for combating it.

The assertion that the death penalty deters crime more effectively than other punishments is now largely discredited by the lack of scientific evidence despite the many studies that have been made. Yet many members of the public believe that it does. Their belief flies in the face of the scientific evidence. In other words, the public does not have a scientific understanding of the deterrent effect of the death penalty.

---

1. Schabas W.A. (1997), *The abolition of the death penalty in international law* (2nd edn) Cambridge, Cambridge University Press, p. 20.

As the United Nations secretariat suggested as long ago as 1980, governments should take on the task of educating the public as to the uncertainty of the deterrent effect of capital punishment (United Nations Document No. A/CONF87/9, paragraph 68). A better public understanding of crime prevention and criminal justice would produce more support for anti-crime measures which are genuine and not merely palliative. At the very least, politicians should not make demagogic calls for the death penalty, misleading the public and obscuring the need for genuine anti-crime measures.

For Amnesty International, the human rights argument is paramount. But in practice, it is only one of several powerful arguments against the death penalty which need to be part of the national debate.

While Amnesty International is making the human rights argument, others need to make the other arguments. Statements from religious leaders, other respected public figures, influential organisations and the news media can create a moral climate in which the legislators will be more willing to vote in a way which they know will be unpopular with many of their constituents.

Often the national debate on the death penalty is conducted in purely national terms. The international dimension needs to be brought in. Countries can learn from other countries' experience.

Over the centuries, laws and public attitudes relating to torture have evolved. It is no longer permissible to use thumbscrews or the rack as legally sanctioned means of interrogation and punishment. Attitudes toward the death penalty are also changing, and as an increasing number of countries abolish capital punishment, the guillotine, the garrotte and the noose are being relegated to the museums, alongside the medieval instruments of torture.

Bringing about abolition requires courageous political leadership, leadership which will be exercised in the defence of human rights. The requirement of respect for human rights has to include the abolition of the death penalty. It is not possible for a government to respect human rights and retain the death penalty at the same time.

2. THE DEATH PENALTY AND THE "FAIRY RING"

Philippe Toussaint, Editor in Chief of the Journal des procès

> *First Witch:* Paddock calls.
> *Second Witch:* Anon.
> *Third witch:* Fair is foul, and foul is fair:
> Hover through the fog and filthy air.
>
> (Shakespeare. *Macbeth*, Act I, Scene I)

The death penalty and execution of capital punishment, which are two different things, the former being able to exist without the latter, are subjects it is always better not to talk about at all. The fact is that they call up what Professor Kellens[1] of the University of Liège calls "a fairy ring", which immediately reduces any discussion to the lowest level, the problem being that, broadly speaking, it would appear that public opinion is in favour of this penalty and of executions, while the reputedly "enlightened" stratum of this public opinion is, with some exceptions, implacably opposed. It is thus a matter of a thorny democratic problem, one of those problems – for there are others – which put many of us in a situation that is difficult because it is contradictory. It puts us in mind of a pronouncement that Plato attributes to Socrates, to the effect that the City should not choose its strategies by the democratic path, the citizens generally not being capable, through incompetence, of deciding who has the qualities required for exercising such functions, so that in certain cases arbitrary, essentially anti-democratic, action is the only way of saving democracy.

In Belgium, my country, for over a century we adopted, as is often the case, a halfway solution through maintaining the death penalty in the Penal Code, while adopting the habit of never applying it, but for a few exceptions. One such exception was in 1917, when the French executioner and a guillotine were brought to the tiny area that had not been occupied by the Germans, for the execution of a condemned man about whom it was said that it would

---

1. Professor of Criminology, University of Liège.

have been scandalous to send him to the safety of a prison while so many honest men were dying heroically in the trenches. Other exceptions, perfectly legal, concerned some three hundred people in 1945, condemned for crimes perpetrated in a context again connected with war, since they had collaborated with the occupying power, denouncing patriots, having Jews sent to extermination camps, etc. It was only recently, in 1996, that the legislature abolished the death penalty.

It is remarkable that for many years the subject was in a way taboo. Political circles were apparently well satisfied with the hypocritical solution consisting of systematically reprieving all persons condemned to death, thus leaving the door open for possible exceptions, for example in the case of war or of crimes so horrible that public opinion might demand what was after all nothing more than the application of the law. People preferred not to think about it. The tragedy of the abducted and murdered children which descended on Belgium three years ago, an earthquake that justifiably continues to shake the Belgians and which underlies far-reaching reforms of the legal system and the police, might well have triggered a reaction in favour of capital punishment. This was not the case however; but for very rare exceptions, even the most ardent partisans of greater repression of criminal paedophilia are willing to settle for prison sentences without possibility of early release. It is something that can be seen as social progress.

If we leave Belgium, we see that it is in the United States that the problems are the most worrying, not only because of the large number of cases of capital punishment, but more fundamentally because it is a country that likes to proclaim its status as the world's leading democracy, in fact as an exemplary democracy. The paradox here is indeed striking, with on the one hand criminal trials conducted with every effort to scrupulously respect the rights of the defence and the presumption of innocence, and on the other the spectacle of capital punishment involving methods of a sinister diversity. A spectacle indeed, because these executions, in public, often give rise to a kind of televised show in which the adversaries of the death penalty never tire of describing the barbarity of these executions in detail. Many Americans are sick of it, and with good reason. On 25 March 1997, for example, Pedro Medina, who had never ceased claiming his innocence of the murder of a woman, and on whose behalf the Pope had intervened, "withstood" an electric shock of 2 000 volts with flames shooting from his head. It was only after several minutes that the victim ceased living. The comment made on this by the Attorney General of Florida, Mr Bob Butterworth, is no doubt worth posting up: "People who want to commit murder better not do it in Florida because we may have a problem with our electric chair. "[1]

---

1. *Le Monde* of 28.03.98 (English version translated back from the French – Trad.).

If I cite this example out of a great number of equally horrifying ones, it is because in a way it sums up most of the elements of the problem that concerns us here. The Pope, in 1997, had not yet advocated the abolition of the death penalty. The new edition of the catechism, revised and corrected by Rome, stipulated in paragraph 2266 that:

> "Preserving the common good of society requires rendering the aggressor unable to inflict harm. For this reason the traditional teaching of the Church has acknowledged as well-founded the right and duty of legitimate public authority to punish malefactors by means of penalties commensurate with the gravity of the crime, not excluding, in cases of extreme gravity, the death penalty. For analogous reasons those holding authority have the right to repel by armed force aggressors against the community in their charge."[1]

One cannot help but compare this text with the comment made on the technically botched execution of Pedro Medina by Attorney General Butterworth, who had remained unmoved by the Pope's intervention, based more on circumstances than on theory. How to discuss with a state attorney who can say such things, how to react without immediately entering into his own game, without descending to his level? This question is all the more embarrassing in that Butterworth could have pointed out that the Pope's intervention was illogical because in a text as official as that of the catechism, his Church recognised the right of public authorities to resort to the death penalty.

The fact is that the issue is clear-cut; looking at it any other way is to fall *ipso facto* into dreadful contradictions. It necessarily escapes dialectic on both sides; one is not for or against the death penalty and capital punishment for such and such a reason, one is simply for or against, exactly in the same way as it cannot be demonstrated without peril, why one is for human rights, the argumentation one would present implying that it would be wrong, for this or that reason, to support the opposite view, which would nevertheless merit examination. It suffices to think of a few examples: is it necessary, and above all is it proper, to demonstrate that torture or rape should be proscribed?

The article[1] by de Béco and Evrard (the latter being a doctoral student at the Pontifical University of Latran, in Rome) ends with this sentence, announcing pretty well the sentiment of the authors: "It is not unreasonable to think that one day, the Catholic Church, through purely and simply condemning

---

1. *"Le Catéchisme de l'Eglise catholique de Rome et la question de la peine de mort – Considérations actuelles au regard des évolutions récentes."* French version taken from an article by E. de Béco and A. Evrard *Journal des procès*, 6 February 1998, pp. 10 ff. English version from the Internet site: home.sprynet.com/sprynet/stever05/Capital.html.

the death penalty, will fully affirm the primacy of the absolute respect of the human person." Things have moved more quickly than de Béco and Evrard thought, than they hoped, no doubt, since the Pope has in his turn become an abolitionist. We can assume that this is because a prudent attitude had become untenable on this issue, without maintaining the "fairy ring " and a debate inevitably shameful for everybody.

Quite a different subject is that of a significant increase in legal repression in the United States, where thirty-nine states practice the death penalty (the Supreme Court having long ago lifted its veto on capital punishment) but where, also, the number of long-term prisoners is proportionally two or three times higher than that in the countries of western Europe. The conditions of detention in the United States are often officially very much harsher than in most reputedly civilised countries (the ball and chain being used on prisoners, for example). We can see very well that repression of crime is of the same origin, with regard to its exemplary value, its effects on crime. It is not easy to draw lessons in this respect. Thus there is no doubt that the crime rate fell very significantly in the state of New York as the result of a spectacular increase in police resources and much stiffer sentences imposed by the courts. Honest citizens, we read in the newspapers, can walk at night in Central Park, without running the risk – a virtual certainty not long ago – of being attacked and robbed or killed. The result is therefore good even if, as always, its cost needs to be examined from different points of view.

I walked more than once in the streets of Moscow at night in the Soviet era, secure as could be. The statistics, for once reliable in this case, revealed only a minute number of crimes and misdemeanours perpetrated in the streets (but a substantially higher number of swindles and frauds of all sorts in the hotels frequented by foreigners). This relative safety from physical violence (things having now changed radically in Moscow, as everybody knows) had a terribly high price, that of camps where people were soon sent for infringing the law. I remember in this connection a trial I followed (through an interpreter) in Moscow in 1982. The defendant was a young man of eighteen who, on the day of the offence concerned, had obtained his heavy vehicle driving licence and celebrated the event with friends. He got drunk and late in the evening, trying to get home and no longer having any more than a single kopeck in his pocket, he had not been able to open the gate of the metro, which cost two. He had jumped over, but was seen by a female official who raised the alarm. He had galloped through the corridors chased by police and, by luck, he thought, had been able to jump into a train just as it was starting to move. The door had closed automatically and he thought he was safe, but in the compartment there were two militiamen who realised what had happened. He was defended with conviction by a delegate from his *komsomol*, his youth organisation, but this had not won the indulgence of the court however, and the prosecutor called for a harsh sentence against this defendant who had, she said, compromised the construction of socialism through his behaviour. He was condemned to two years in a camp with the "ordinary" regime. At this level repression becomes effective.

In this same period I visited the Moscow Institute of Criminology. Here it was admitted that most unfortunately they had scarcely any criminal statistics, which made the work of the criminologists somewhat useless. The Ministry of the Interior communicated reassuring figures on street crime, but not, in particular, on the number of executions, which could only be worked out by reading the newspapers, where these events were reported more or less regularly. Thus nothing was certain scientifically, but this perhaps only strengthened the feeling of security that the authorities wished to foster. It was known that there were many death sentences, many executions by firing squad, and it was not necessary to know in what precise cases the sentences had been pronounced, or in what sorts of cases, for the population to be convinced that the smallest offence would be cracked down on with extreme severity.

Things are not so simple in the United States, where the criminal statistics are kept with care. We know very precisely how many condemned prisoners were executed in the state of Arizona in a given year, in how many states execution is by lethal injection, how many hangings there are elsewhere, how many electrocutions, etc. there have been. This is even what, at one and the same time, arouses a certain hope among the abolitionists and pushes another section of public opinion to desire the maintenance of the system. The former imagine that so many horrors, meticulously and irrefutably described, will end up by revolting the partisans of the death penalty, while the latter on the contrary see it as a demonstration of how order is properly defended. There is no option for either side but to bank on an increase in the number of executions.

If I dwell on the situation in the United States concerning the death penalty, this is because the example set by the world's largest democracy is obviously disastrous for the countries moving towards democracy, or claiming to be. I am thinking in particular of China, where as we all know, though precise figures are not available, that a large number of condemned persons are executed, with the shameful scandal of organs being taken from the bodies immediately after "justice has been done", to be sold abroad at enormous prices. This is in fact not without interest for the adversaries of the death penalty. Barbarity can but lead to further barbarity, a vicious spiral that is likely to end in an insupportable explosion of atrocities, but when? It would follow on from the logic adopted, for example, that one day wealthy tourists will be offered the opportunity – for a high price – of watching executions and that the spectacle, in order to attract more spectators, will be given extra spice by a little preliminary torture. Nobody can say how far things will go.

I am in any event convinced that one day things will change all of a sudden. As in Belgium, after over a century in which Article 8 of the Penal Code stated that "Any person condemned to death shall have his head cut off," it was abolished by the law of 10 July 1996. Very suddenly and practically without debate the position was reversed, public opinion having registered the fact without reaction.

It will be the same, this is my hope, in the United States and then in other countries where capital punishment is still practised. Countries regress in this field only all the better to renounce their position in great haste, as if it were first necessary to attain a certain degree of horror before abolishing the death penalty.

3. VICTIMS OF CRIME AND THE DEATH PENALTY

Peter Hodgkinson, Director – Centre for Capital Punishment Studies, School of Law, University of Westminster

"In Media, Pennsylvania, at least once a week Gail Willard makes a pilgrimage to a highway off-ramp in suburban Philadelphia. With cars zooming by, the 48-year-old nurse sits on the guard-rail and gazes at two simple crosses, one she made and one made by her ex-husband. There she ponders painfully the twelve-mile journey her daughter Aimee took from that spot to a drug-ravaged North Philadelphia ghetto where an identical cross stands.

In the two years since her youngest child's raped and beaten body was found in a trash strewn vacant lot, Ms Willard has become an advocate for murder victims, a witness for parole reform and a troubled figure at the centre of a debate on the death penalty. Now with the college ring of her lacrosse-playing daughter on her hand she is bracing for the trial of Arthur J. Bomar, the alleged killer, who had been paroled after serving time for murder in Nevada. Aimee's empty car was found on the off-ramp at about 2 a.m. on 20 June 1996. Whilst home from George Mason University in Fairfax, Virginia, visiting her mother the 22-year-old had vanished sometime while driving back from a reunion with friends at a bar the evening before.

Police who found the blue Honda Civic were baffled; the door was open, the engine was running, the lights and radio were on. The driver might have just stepped away, officers thought. Then they noticed the blood on the asphalt. The next day young boys found Aimee's body, naked, beaten and run over by a car in a weed-choked, trash strewn vacant lot – a world away from her life in the quiet suburb of Brookhaven. An autopsy revealed the killer had raped her and then crushed her skull. A year later, in June 1997, Bomar was picked up for a burglary, driving the car of a Philadelphia woman who had been missing since March. Police decided to question him about the Willard slaying. In December whilst in prison for burglary he was charged with Aimee's murder. According to the affidavit, sperm taken from Aimee's body matched Bomar's DNA, his car tyres matched tread marks on the body and bruises on her body corresponded to ridges on his car's oil pan on the bottom of the car.

He was also charged with kidnapping, rape and abuse of a corpse. At the time of the murder Bomar was on parole to the state of Nevada where he had served twelve years of a life-sentence for shooting a man over a parking space. This time prosecutors are determined he never leaves prison again. 'We are responsible for representing the state and we are going to do our job – which means trying to put Bomar on death row', says Delaware County District Attorney Patrick Meehan. At the end of August Pennsylvania had 214 men and four women on death row.

Gail Willard believes Bomar killed her daughter but as a devout Roman Catholic and death penalty opponent she is pitted against prosecutors over his potential sentence. 'I'm not snuffing out the life of a prisoner. It's morally reprehensible,' she says. 'I don't want to see his mother suffer as well.' She says that she is more concerned to fix the system that freed him. She keeps a long list in her shirt pocket of meetings with reporters and community leaders from across the country all seeking her views on Bomar's release on parole. She began the list within days of Bomar's arrest. Her inspiration is the suspect's glare. 'When he glances at us in the courtroom I feel his evil. I know I'm in the presence of it,' says Ms Willard's sister, Sister Nancy Bonshock, a nun and teacher at Aimee's high school. She has been Gail Willard's constant companion during the pre-trial hearings. For the last year they have sat stunned listening to court-room accounts of the hellish last hours of Aimee's life.

'It still hurts when I realise how Aimee must have suffered at this man's hands. I just want to scream when I hear the stories that come out in the courtroom.' Ms Willard has made a special videotape in hopes that prosecutors and jurors will see her daughter as she was – the baby of the family, a popular student at George Mason, a soccer and All-American lacrosse player whose body was identified by the tattoo of the Nike logo on her leg. At a coffee shop blocks away from the courthouse where Bomar has pleaded not guilty, tears well in her eyes when she speaks her daughter's name. She clears her throat to compose herself and tells how she fights despair by focusing on reform not revenge. Sometimes she takes a lawn chair to the cemetery and sits with her daughter, chatting to her and praying for a conviction.

She and her sister plan to be in court every day, starting Monday when jury selection begins 220 miles away in Westmoreland County, just east of Pittsburgh. Common Pleas Court Judge Frank Hazel hopes that jurors 'imported' from western Pennsylvania will be unbiased. The trial will take place in Media.

'I was at everything that Aimee did when she was alive. I'm not going to miss anything now'."[1]

This chapter reviews some of the issues raised when the debate about homicide victims and their friends' and families' needs is engaged. The author is continuing research on the topic and a fuller account will be published in a forthcoming book *The Death Penalty: a collection of essays on strategies for abolition*, edited by himself and Professor William A. Schabas. In the main, this chapter will reflect the debate as illustrated by practice in the United Kingdom and the United States.

It is my belief that victims of crime represent a major omission from the rhetoric of the abolitionist community. Few, if any, such groups make a conscious effort to express explicit concern for the victims of crime assuming their concern is taken as read. Sadly nothing could be further from the truth as even a cursory examination of victims and those groups which provide support for victims will bear witness. I believe that most victims' groups see the "penal reform" industry as being wholly on the side of the offender and therefore by implication indifferent to the needs and rights of victims. It is for this reason that in the United States there has been an almost exponential rise in victims' groups whose primary objective seems to be the pursuit of harsh penalties rather than their more traditional role of providing emotional and practical support for victims. The accent seems too to be on rights rather than needs though necessarily some needs should be met as a matter of right.

The United Kingdom too has experienced a sea change in the victims' movement with a multiplicity of groups competing with Victim Support, the founding victims' group in the United Kingdom,[2] not just for funds but for

---

1. From Associated Press as reported on Rick Halperin's Death Penalty News Site 14 September 1998. I selected this piece of reporting, not because it was particularly remarkable, as sadly it is typical of the daily reports illustrating an out of control violence in US society. In a population of 260 million there are on average some 20 000 plus murders annually as contrasted with the UK which records on average some 650 murders annually in a population of 56 million. What this article does illustrate is the issue of the plight of the victim herself, the effect on the immediate family, the wishes of the family and the prosecutor's position. Furthermore the mother's wish to submit a Victim Impact Statement, not for the purpose of influencing the sentence, but with the intention of having her daughter "brought to life" and her memory respected. One wonders whether the victim support network in Media assisted with the provision of access to counselling and as importantly whether any financial support was given to enable this mother to attend court throughout the proceedings.

2. The National Association of Victim Support Schemes (NAVSS now Victim Support) had its origins in the initiative prompted by the National Association for the Care and Resettlement of Offenders (NACRO) which founded The Bristol Victim-Offenders Group in 1969. This group developed strategies to work with the victims of personal crime referred to them by the police. They established a multidisciplinary team of professionals who trained volunteers. This group eventually formed into the Bristol Victim Support Scheme in 1974. Similar groups began to form countrywide and the NAVSS was formed in 1979.

public and government support of their ideologies. A criticism voiced by some of these new arrivals is that Victim Support must inevitably compromise its position, and therefore the needs and rights of victims, because it is largely dependant on the government for funding. Victim Support for its part has always taken the line not to campaign in the area of punishment, in fact its constitution bars it from so doing save in the area of compensation. In contrast some of the new organisations, aping their United States' counterparts, have very aggressive campaigns for stiffer penalties and the establishment of procedural rights for victims. These "rights" include Victim Impact Statements; active participation in the sentencing process; involvement in any decision-making forum where early release is being considered and finally the right to know when "their" offender is being released from prison and where s/he is living. A far cry from the days when the needs of victims were provided by local volunteers who helped with such "mundane" activities as providing a sympathetic ear, contacting builders to repair damage to property, helping to allay fear of re-victimisation, contacting friends and relatives, and finding temporary accommodation.[1] Victim Support has never seen its volunteers as professional counsellors preferring to refer on to others for such professional help whilst concentrating its energies lobbying on behalf of traditional victim needs and supporting and initiating schemes directed at making the criminal justice system less frightening and more accessible to victims. Examples of this are projects such as Witnesses at Court, improving victim relations with the prosecuting authorities, lobbying for separate facilities for victims and their families at court.[2] It has also promoted research into victim needs and effective measures to meet those needs. For example, special projects have been established to respond to families of murdered children and to the victims of rape. Once these pilot schemes are up and running and evaluated the statutory and voluntary sector is invited to assume responsibility for their continuation and expansion nationwide. On the whole Victim Support has been successful in meeting its objectives over the last twenty-five years without needing to engage in aggressive political campaigns demanding "rights" for victims.[3] Undoubtedly the decision to produce a Victim's Charter in 1990 and 1996 was directly the result of the quiet, behind the scenes lobbying that characterises the approach of Victim Support[4] though the 1996 version did owe much of its

1. Holtom, C. and Raynor, P. (1988), "Origins of victim support: philosophy and practice" in M. Maguire and J. Pointing, Eds. *Victims of Crime: a new deal?* Milton Keynes. Open University Press (1988).
2. Rock, Paul (1991), The Victim in Court Project at the Crown Court at Wood Green. *Howard Journal*, Vol. 30 No. 4 pp. 301-310.
3. Rock, Paul (1990), *Helping victims of crime: The Home Office and the rise of victim support in England and Wales*. Oxford.
4. Home Office (1990), *Victim's Charter: a Statement of the Rights of Victims*. London, HMSO.

rhetoric to the influence of the more vocal lobbyists and the populist susceptibility of the then Home Secretary, Michael Howard.[1]

Many decades of research have improved our knowledge of the experiences and needs of victims.[2] From von Hentig's work in the 1940s,[3] which raised the notion of victim precipitation arguing that there were characteristics inherent in some who became victims which led to their victimisation – subsequent research in this area suggested that victims were in some way to "blame" for their predicament. The 1960s saw the arrival of "victim survey"[4] research in the United States and the United Kingdom, which in turn spawned the British Crime Surveys,[5] which have in recent years provided valuable information about the perceptions victims have of the criminal justice process. The core issues identified from this research, of importance to victims, are fear of crime, anger and frustration, loss of confidence and at the extremes there are victims whose suffering is so severe that it amounts to a clinical condition.[6] There is one myth that needs debunking immediately and that is the perception among some researchers that victims of crime are a homogeneous group with identical needs susceptible to similar solutions.

Over the past decade or so there has been a growth of victims groups, many of which have developed in response to the plight of individual victims or particular crimes. The Suzy Lamplugh Trust and the Zito Trust were both established by family members in the hopes that others may learn from the mistakes that led to their loved ones suffering. They set out to create a climate of understanding through which change could be encouraged – the

1. Michael Howard, the then Home Secretary launched this document in June of 1996. The byword was "giving victims a voice" and it was set out to make quite specific undertakings to victims – perhaps more "rights" orientated than "needs". The main tenets of the Charter are: provision of information to victims; taking victims' views into account; treating victims with respect and sensitivity at court; and providing support to victims.
2. Shapland, J., Willmore, J., and Duff, P. (1985), *Victims and the Criminal Justice System*. Aldershot, Gower. Maguire, M. and Corbett, C. (1987), *The Effects of Crime and the Work of Victim Support Schemes*. Aldershot, Gower.
3. von Hentig, H., *The Criminal and his Victim* (New York: 1948).
4. Sparks, R., Genn, H. and Dodd, D. (1977), *Victims and the Criminal Justice System*. Oxford, Wiley Press.
5. The first British Crime Survey was published in 1983 and has been repeated six times (1985, 1989, 1992, 1994, 1996 and 1998). The original conception was an attempt to provide an alternative and hopefully more accurate picture of the nature and volume of crime than that provided by the official statistics collected by the police forces. Over the years it has evolved and in addition to refining its statistical accuracy it has established an agenda of data collection and research which highlights the experiences and perceptions of victims which has led to initiatives which attempt to meet the identified needs of victims. This model has also been used in discrete local areas where its results have directly influenced crime prevention and policies on victims' needs.
6. For a full description of these issues and a general review of the victim debate see *Victims of Crime* a briefing paper prepared by the Howard League for Penal Reform in 1997: 708 Holloway Road, London N19 3NL, Tel: +44 (0) 171 281 7722.

change in the case of the Lamplugh Trust was to the procedures of estate agents[1] to ensure that no female staff attends such appointments unaccompanied. Jayne Zito's husband Jonathan was killed, whilst waiting at a railway station, by Christopher Clunis who had recently been discharged from mental health care, it later transpired without support or medication. Her campaign for a public enquiry[2] was successful and the trust she founded has become active and influential on such issues as community care for the mentally ill and the needs of the victims of assault by the mentally ill. I use these two to illustrate the capacity to divert the pain of bereavement, in such circumstances, from destructive outcomes into creative outcomes, believing that such an approach has benefits for the families of victims and society in general.

The abolitionist community might attract some sympathy for their agenda if they promoted policies that helped establish a climate where respect for victims and their families is at least of equal importance as ensuring the legal and civil rights of the accused and the condemned. Jayne Zito drawing on her background in mental health coupled with a working knowledge of the criminal justice system was able to put this to use and this perhaps helped her, in her words, to avoid "a destructive pattern of grief".

As mentioned above other organisations, such POMC[3] (Parents of Murdered Children), SAMM[4] (Support after Murder and Manslaughter) developed in response to particular crimes. Some developing from within existing groups have established independence, Justice for Victims is one such group.

This brief review is undertaken to set the context for the discussion of the development of responses to the needs of victims of crime and to their families and the influence they have on the debate about punishment, in this instance capital punishment. Paul Rock in his recent defining work *After Homicide*[5] explains what brought him to undertake his analysis:

---

1. Suzy Lamplugh disappeared after keeping an appointment alone with a male client, who had ostensibly arranged to view a property – there has been no trace of her since then (1986).
2. North East and South East Thames Regional Health Authorities, *The Report of the Inquiry into the Care and Treatment of Christopher Clunis* (1994). London HMSO.
3. Parents of Murdered Children was established in 1990 as a separate group which had its origins in The Compassionate Friends (TCP) set up in 1969. In 1980, TCF and POMC became a joint organisation. Out of POMC sprang the Victims of Crime Pressure Group (1993) and Families of Murder Victims (1993).
4. SAMM, which was formed out of POMC in 1994, experienced some conflict of direction in its early days when a sub-group Justice for Victims (1994) formed from among its membership. Justice for Victims had and continues to have some antipathy towards Victim Support, which harmed the relationship SAMM had with them. The current relationship is more positive as SAMM have an office in Victim Support premises and they collaborate on a number of issues.
5. Rock, Paul (1998), *After Homicide*. Oxford, Clarendon Press.

"Work on this book was prompted by a general and long-standing inter-est in policy-making for victims of crime, on the one hand, and, on the other, by a more specific awareness that things seemed to be stirring in the politics of victims of homicide and violence in the mid-1990s."

He went on to say,

"It [his research] looks at victims' organisations striving to reassert mean-ing and control in a world that has been turned upside down. There are distinctive symbolic procedures at work, which must be understood before the politics and practices of these groups become transparent. Without such a grasp, it would be all too simple to dismiss many of the people as marginal, unreasonable, unnecessary, and aggressive; to despatch them, in the manner of a number of established institutions in the criminal justice system, as mere 'angry victims', or to talk, as one article[1] put it, of the 'increasingly strident demands of fringe organisations like Justice for Victims'."

Rock's enquiry charts the development of the victims' movement, its rela-tionship to its constituents, to other group members, to the general public and finally to central government. Whilst his work focuses on the United Kingdom, the influence that the victim movement in the United States has had and continues to have on the debate within the movement in the United Kingdom is obvious to see. At the risk of over-simplifying the debate it seems to me that the principal thrust of many new groups is concern for severe punishment and more procedural rights for victims to influence the outcome of actions against offenders. This approach has struck a rich vein of approval amongst the public, the tabloid press and politicians on the right (and some on the left) and furthermore there is evidence that it is having an impact shaping policy on the ground locally and centrally through legislation.

An example of this is the public concern expressed when individuals con-victed of sexual offences against children are released from prison. Specifically, demands are made for the resettlement plans and locations of such offenders to be disclosed and on those occasions when such informa-tion has been leaked it has led, predictably, to the formation of vigilante groups, which hound out such individuals. This leaves the problem with the police who have to take them temporarily into protective custody whilst more permanent and suitable plans are devised. This development is in itself deeply worrying but more so is the evidence that legislators are being per-suaded to contemplate new legislation placing more restrictions on the movements, and therefore individual rights, of people who have formally

---

1. Casey, S. (1995), "Victims' Rights", *Oxford Today*, Hilary 1995, Vol. 7, No. 2, p. 24.

paid their debts to society. Changes under consideration are the inclusion of such people in newly formulated mental health legislation and the reintroduction of the reviewable sentence. Whilst adequate safeguards are essential to ensure public safety a balance has to be struck between the needs and rights of potential future victims and the needs and rights of offenders. Such public disclosure will have the effect of driving such individuals underground where they will escape any supervision. This particular victims' "right" has been influenced by developments in the United States[1] and there is little doubt that Michael Howard's decision[2] in principle and in practice to consign a number of life-sentenced prisoners to a natural life sentence was in direct response to the lobbying of certain victims' groups. In the view of some, the rise in retributive punishment is the direct responsibility of the modern victims' movement, an outcome mirroring the developments in the United States. Pat Carlen[3] for one believes that:

> "The final strand in the new punitiveness is the rise and rise of the crime victim. Since the mid-1970s there has been a growing emphasis on the neglect and invisibility of the victim of crime in the administration of justice. The trumpeting of crime-victim wrongs has been useful to anyone wishing to make an electoral appeal on law and order issues. Although at a commonsense level one might have thought that it is because crimes do have victims that anyone ever cared about crime in the first place, the 1970s rediscovery of the victim has certainly fed into the 1990s punitiveness – and with a vengeance! The results? A greatly increased fear of crime, daily demands for stiffer sentences, and a steep increase in levels of criminological nonsense."

There is evidence from the United Kingdom and the United States that the focus of many victims groups, especially newly formed ones, is on campaigning for severe sanctions, increased restrictions on offenders and more

---

1. Megan's Law is legislation named after Megan Kanka, the 7-year-old who was raped and killed by Jesse Timmendequas. On 29 July 1994, Timmendequas lured Megan into his house across the street from her to see his puppy where he killed her. The next day he led police to the body in a nearby park. After the murder it was disclosed to her parents and neighbours that he had two previous sex convictions against children and had been moved into that area after being released from prison. Her parents campaigned for laws to require that neighbours be notified when sex offenders move into an area. New Jersey passed legislation, which came into effect on 31 October 1994, followed by most other states. President Clinton enacted a federal law in 1996. CNN Plus web site.
2. Michael Howard, was the former British Home Secretary who identified seventeen life-sentenced prisoners for whom he would not exercise his discretion for early release implying that they would serve natural life sentences. He also increased the tariff from eight to fifteen years for the two 10-year-olds convicted of the murder of 2½-year-old Jamie Bulger. This decision has been successfully challenged in the domestic and European courts.
3. Carlen, Pat. *Jigsaw: a political criminology of youth homelessness*, Open University Press, Milton Keynes, 1996, p.53.

procedural rights. This, despite the fact that there is little evidence to suggest that longer sentences lead to a more effective sentencing policy or that victims benefit. The only people to benefit from this approach would appear to be politicians and lobbyists arguably at the expense of victims' vulnerability, being further exposed and exploited.

Now to the main purpose of this chapter, the victim movement in the United States and its influence on the capital punishment debate. The United States has the distinction of being the only western industrial democracy that retains and uses the death penalty. There are over 3 500 inmates on death rows across the United States in thirty-eight states, in federal government institutions and the military prisons of which number roughly 54% are minorities, 98% are adult men and approximately 3% are juveniles. The modern era of capital punishment signalled by the landmark United States Supreme Court decision in *Gregg v. Georgia* (1976)[1] has seen 500 executions – the 500th execution took place in South Carolina on 18 December 1998.

The major co-ordinating group for homicide victims in the United States, the National Organisation of Parents of Murdered Children, Incorporated (NOPOMC)[2] has its beginnings in the early 1970s and like many such groups in the United States, is rooted in the rights-based model unlike Victim Support in the United Kingdom. NOPOMC and similar groups owe their origins to the right in politics and consider that an important need of victims is the right to procedural intervention in the criminal justice system including the determination of sentence. Many such groups, which are allied with movements to retain or restore the death penalty, benefit from their connections with politicians and prosecutors and given the populist nature of American politics are well placed to influence penal policy at the ballot box. This power is significant given that the main players in the legal system are elected officials and many victims' groups have representatives located in offices adjacent to those of the Attorney General and district attorneys whose confidence and support they enjoy. They are very influential in

---

1. *Gregg v. Georgia* (1976), 428 U.S. 153.
2. The NOPOMC was founded in 1978 and now co-ordinates a confederation of 300 groups across the USA and receives over 100 000 requests for assistance annually. It publishes, nationally, a newsletter *Survivor*, which informs its membership about the activities of the national and state branches. Reports of changes to legislation and practice that affect victims, updates on personal stories of victimisation, a letters page, the Parole Block campaign and MINE (Murder Is Not Entertainment) are regular features. Recent issues have addressed support for the campaign to introduce a Victims' Rights Amendment to the US Constitution. Parole Block is a campaign to support families and friends of homicide victims objecting to the release on parole of "their" murderer. MINE is a campaign to persuade the entertainment industry to treat the topic of murder with sensitivity. Some state variations include in their brief "other survivors of homicide victims". NOPOMC, 100 East Eighth St., B-41 Cincinnati, Ohio 45202, Tel: (513) 721-5683 (http://www.pomc.com/origin.html).

shaping some aspects of penal policy and their power rests not only in influencing particular pieces of legislation but more insidiously in dictating the agenda and the rhetoric about capital punishment shamelessly exploiting their status as relatives of murder victims – a very strong emotional appeal indeed.

An early difficulty to be faced by the victim world was that of nomenclature – what do you call a person who is related to a homicide victim and furthermore how near or far in lineage can you go and still claim this close relationship to the deceased? Should one restrict this association to immediate family, to non-married live-in partners, to heterosexual and homosexual relationships, to intimate friends? Who decides? Unlike other types of victims, homicide victims have no further involvement in the process of criminal justice and this function is assumed by the state and occasionally by their nearest and dearest. Terms that have been adopted and used interchangeably are "secondary victim", "in-visible victim", "co-victim" and more recently "survivor". In my opinion none of these accurately describe the person or persons directly affected by those who mourn the loss of the victim, who may or may not be a family member and who may not in fact be suffering from the loss. It seems to me, long-winded though it is, that the most appropriate description is a functional one, namely, "family and friends of the deceased". In any event why should it make any difference how you label those known to the victim? The reason is that in the political climate of the victims' movement a label reflects status and the rights that flow from this official recognition – such as the right:

- to economic and emotional support;
- to be informed about the progress of the police investigation;
- to be present at trial;
- to provide information at the sentencing phase (Victim Impact Statement);
- to receive compensation from the state and/or from the condemned;
- to be consulted about the sentence – life or death;
- to be consulted at clemency and parole hearings;
- to be present at the execution.

As mentioned above the struggle in the United States is going to be that much harder because of the populist nature of its democracy where most key legal and criminal justice personnel are elected and therefore vulnerable to the vagaries of public opinion. Sadly recent history has shown a distinct lack of moral fibre in those seeking office who follow or hide behind public opinion rather than lead it, which is contrary to the experience in the United Kingdom since abolition in 1965. The apologist would argue that the only way for "liberals" to gain political office is to espouse tough law and order strategies and then when in office to gradually reveal their inherent liberal self. There is little evidence to suggest that President Clinton, who came to office on the execution of a mentally ill and retarded inmate Ricky Ray Rector, is about to reveal his liberal tendencies.

Not all is doom and gloom in the United States as a significant counter to the pro-punishment, pro-revenge victim lobby is provided by the organisations, Murder Victims' Families for Reconciliation[1] and the Journey of Hope. Both organisations share similar beliefs and constituents, the latter having evolved from the former, as all are families or friends of victims of homicide and passionately opposed to the death penalty.

An inherent contradiction and injustice in a victim-driven criminal justice system is illustrated by the two approaches reflected above with respect to those convicted of capital murder. If all victims' wishes are to be respected then prosecutions for capital murder would be even more inconsistent than at present – one simply cannot have a prosecution policy based on the wishes of the families and friends of homicide victims, where some are for and some against capital punishment. There is evidence that prosecutors do take the wishes of victims' families into account, though it appears that the majority of such families and such wishes are pro-death penalty.[2] There is evidence too that irrespective of their individual inclinations the agenda of such groups, actively supported by the prosecution industry, is pro-punishment and pro-revenge – they feed on anger and hate.

This practice of a victim-driven prosecution and sentencing policy is evident in many other parts of the world, none more so than in those countries where Sharia law applies. Depending on local variations in interpretation and practice victims' families have the right to determine whether the condemned is sentenced to death, choose the mode of execution (beheading or stoning – though in some jurisdictions the mode is determined by the

---

1. Marie Deans following the murder of her mother-in-law founded Murder Victims Families for Reconciliation (MVFR) in Virginia. MVFR was founded to provide a national forum for murder victims' family members, including family members of those executed by the state, who are opposed to the death penalty. Later with the help of Marietta Jaeger, whose daughter was murdered, MVFR expanded its movement throughout the states. In Indiana in 1993 the first Journey of Hope was staged and this has been followed with marches throughout a variety of states every year since.
2. *Houston Chronicle*, 8 June 1998. Letter from Charles A. Sage whose sister Marilyn was murdered in 1993. He reflects on the meeting with prosecutors and family members before the trial when he suggested that acceptance of a life sentence for a defendant already dying of Aids was the sensible choice. "My view was dismissed by the prosecutors (part of the cottage industry of the death penalty) and by most, but certainly not all, members of the family. The entire process focuses attention on those survivors who favour the death penalty and dismisses opponents. Sanctimonious victims' rights groups court only supporters of the death penalty and ensure that theirs is the only viewpoint quoted by the press." What this letter also highlights is which view and which family member should represent the views of the deceased. Is there a hierarchy of family members and their influence?

offence), demand financial compensation as an alternative to choosing death and finally in some Islamic states the victim's family has the right to be or choose the executioner. Neither the United States nor the Islamic approach meets two essential elements of natural justice, namely consistency and proportionality. Another potential flaw in this process and one that bears on the importance of status is that all these negotiations are undertaken on behalf of the victim, by the state and by the families and friends, begging the question as to whether the procedure of the "living will" should carry weight at the prosecution and the sentencing stage. There are individuals in the United States who have notarised declarations stating that in the event that they are murdered the state should not seek the death penalty – should prosecutors respect that wish or should the state or for that matter the family have the right to override that wish?[1] If the move is towards a victim-driven system then it follows that the victim's view should be more influential than either that of the state or the family and friends.

Following *Lockett v. Ohio* (1978)[2] the defence team in a capital case is allowed to introduce any information sympathetic to the defendant in mitigation. The prosecution is permitted only to introduce evidence relevant to one or other of the aggravating characteristics of the offence. Prosecutors and victims' groups believing this leads to an imbalance sought to address this by making similar provision for the deceased, the victim. Victim Impact evidence was first raised in 1987 in *Booth v. Maryland* (1987)[3] when information, showing the pain and loss suffered by surviving relatives and friends of a murder victim, was offered in support of the prosecution's argument for a death sentence. This was declared inadmissible by the United States Supreme Court. This judgment was overturned by *Payne v. Tennessee* (1991)[4] when the Supreme Court ruled that the prosecution might now introduce evidence to show the victim in a favourable light. Inevitably this process is raw with emotion, antagonistic to the defendant, explicitly a demand for the death penalty and not subject to cross-examination by the defence. Hardly the ideal environment to tease fact from fiction, relevance from irrelevance or to ensure objectivity in sentencing especially when the

---

1. *Boston Globe*, 7 July 1998. Mario Cuomo, who was for three terms Governor of New York state, has attached such a notarised codicil to his will. It reads: "I hereby declare that should I die as a result of a violent crime, I request that the person or persons found guilty for my killing not be subject to or put in jeopardy of the death penalty under any circumstances, no matter how heinous their crime or how much I have suffered." The campaign in New York was started by Sister Camille D'Arienzo in 1994 during the governor's election when it seemed certain that the death penalty would be returning to New York state after an absence of some thirty years. She says that at least 10 000 people across the country have signed statements like Cuomo's.
2. *Lockett v. Ohio*, 438 U.S. 586 (1978).
3. *Booth v. Maryland*, 482 U.S. 496 (1987).
4. *Payne v. Tennessee*, 501 U.S. 808 (1991).

prosecutor and the judge are likely to be elected officials and when in most states juries decide the sentence. Hugo Bedau, critical of this development remarked:

> "Criminal desert is supposed to be measured by the offender's culpability and the harm caused by the crime ... while in theory the harm caused in crimes such as arson or robbery will vary with the value of the property destroyed or money stolen, the harm caused in criminal homicide is deemed uniform in all cases, on the tacit ground that all human lives are of equal worth... Now, however, it will be up to each capital trial jury to decide for itself whether the murder of which the defendant has been found guilty is deserving of a death penalty because of some special features about the victim, features not defined by any statute, possibly not evident to the defendant at the time of the crime, and not specifiable by the trial court or in any uniform manner from case to case."[1]

Not all states permit the Victim Impact Statement (VIS), New York state's recently drafted death penalty statute specifically prohibit the VIS in cases where the death penalty is under consideration whereas the defence can produce in mitigation all manner of "evidence" attesting to the appalling circumstances in which the defendant was brought up – these heart-rending tales are proffered without opportunity for rebuttal. I mention this not in support of the introduction of the VIS in New York state but to point out what is viewed by prosecutors and victims' groups as a serious flaw in the drafting of the legislation which in their view fails to recognise the needs and rights of homicide victims and those who survive them. The balance that has to be achieved is to give recognition to the victim in a respectful and dignified manner while still maintaining objectivity in the legal process. The trial is not the place to consider the very legitimate needs and rights of the families and friends of the victim; there should in effect be a separate Victim Justice System.[2]

The last topic to be addressed in this chapter is that of the burgeoning practice which permits the families and friends of homicide victims to witness the execution of "their" murderer. The decision to extend this "right" to those who survive the victim was arrived at after vigorous campaigning by the victims' lobby and is justified on the grounds that this practice is permitted for those chosen by the condemned and provides an invaluable opportunity to the families and friends of victims for "closure".

---

1. Bedau, Hugo Adam (1994), "American Populism and the Death Penalty: Witnesses at an execution", *Howard Journal of Criminal Justice*, Vol. 33, November, pp. 289-303.
2. See Howard League proposals in their briefing paper *Victims of Crime* available from the League's offices 708 Holloway Road, London N19 3NL, Tel: +44 (0) 171 281 7722.

Thirteen states have provision for victims' families to witness executions[1] with each state having different regulations governing numbers, status, age and dress code. In all states the victims' witnesses are segregated from the witnesses for the condemned and practice is very varied between states as to the preparation and support, before, during and after, for all witnesses.

Why the remaining twenty-five states do not currently have provision for victims' families to witness or why some states do not permit the family of the condemned to witness executions is unclear though hopefully will be made more clear when the author has completed his research into witnesses to execution. Permitting, even encouraging, already pained and vulnerable people to watch while someone is put to death by hanging, lethal injection, lethal gas, firing squad or electrocution is a measure that should not have been implemented without extensive research into the reasons for and the effects of such an experience. I am not aware that there has been much authoritative research conducted and can only conclude that this "right" is a cynical expedience to provide a particular kind of victims' group with another "trophy" to demonstrate its effectiveness.

The general question about how this experience affects all witnesses is also poorly researched but the anecdotal evidence and the testimony of numbers of prison personnel such as the former Warden of Parchman penitentiary in Mississippi, Don Cabana[2] and abolitionists such as Sister Helen Prejean[3] would suggest that significant ill-effects are experienced by many of those who have exposure to the raft of procedures involved in the process of capital punishment. Research conducted involving the media witnesses at the execution of Robert Alton Harris in California in 1992 indicated a range of psychological ill-effects experienced by some of those witnesses. The researchers concluded that, "the experience of being an eyewitness to an execution was associated with the development of dissociative symptoms in several journalists".[4]

---

1. Oklahoma and Washington guarantee families the right to watch. In addition California, Florida, Illinois, Louisiana, Montana, North Carolina, Ohio, Pennsylvania, Texas, Utah and Virginia hold hearings to determine access. Numbers permitted access varies from state to state as does the family status of witnesses. Illinois allows families to watch only through closed-circuit television. It seems that not all states have the same minimum age for witnesses – Missouri does not permit those under the age of 21. Ironic really that one is not old enough to witness an execution at 21 but old enough at 16 to be executed.
2. Cabana, Donald A. (1996), *Death at Midnight: The Confession of an Executioner.* Northeastern University Press: Boston.
3. Prejean, Sister Helen (1993), *Dead Man Walking: An eyewitness account of the death penalty in the United States.* New York, Random House.
4. Freinkel, A., Koopman, C. and Spiegel, D., "Dissociative Symptoms in Media Eyewitnesses of an Execution", *Am J Psychiatry*, Vol. 151, pp. 1335-39.

The author's preliminary research in this area has focused on the process in Texas where the provision for victims' families to witness executions was brought into effect on 26 September 1995. When a proposal to introduce such a measure failed to get legislative time it provoked an outcry amongst the victims' movement and the decision to proceed with the provision by the simple expedient of amending the prison rules with authority from the Attorney General was agreed.[1] Our planned research into witnesses to executions pre-dated this provision and one of the areas of interest to us was whether there were any procedures in place to offer support before, during and after, to those witnessing the execution.

The state of Texas is interesting in this respect because as well as being infamous for its enthusiastic support of the death penalty it has in place a number of projects worthy of further examination. When the state decided to permit the families and friends of victims to witness executions it initiated a victim witness preparation process under the auspices of the Assistant Director of the Victim Services Division, Dan Guerra. In addition to providing information by way of literature to victim witnesses, victim services staff visit prospective witnesses to discuss the execution process and to provide a personal point of contact for the family when they arrive for the execution. A "support room" is set aside in the administration offices in Huntsville for the victim witnesses and it is here that they wait before and return to after the execution. It is now the practice for a representative of victim services to accompany the witness at the execution and afterwards at the meeting with the post-trauma support team.

Each witness is contacted several weeks after the execution to see if they have experienced any emotional or physical problems in the interim.[2] Further assessment of likely ill-effects is being undertaken by the social work programme of the University of Texas at El Paso but it is still too early to analyse the results. The literature provided by the Victim Services Division avoids any comment about the purpose of this particular victims' right though the most frequently quoted justification is that it provides "closure" for the family and friends of victims and, more importantly, it is what they want.

---

1. The Texas Department of Criminal Justice adopted Rule 152.51 concerning authorised witnesses to the execution of an inmate sentenced to death. The rule authority is the Code of Criminal Procedure, Article 43.20, and Attorney General's Letter Opinion No. 95-059 (26 September 1995). Specifically, those persons authorised to witness the execution of an inmate sentenced to death include close relatives of the deceased victim(s).
2. A report dated 28 August 1998 indicates that "For the most part, the majority that have been interviewed have expressed no regrets in their decision to view and did not suffer any post-trauma symptoms." Dan Guerra, Assistant Director, Texas Department of Criminal Justice, Victim Services Division, PO Box 13401, Austin, Texas 78711. Tel: +1 (512) 406 5427.

A number of commentators, I was one, raised some concerns when this "right" was extended to victims' families and friends and it is heartening to note that many of those concerns have been addressed. My major difficulty with this initiative, notwithstanding the rights or wrongs in principle, is that such individuals should be protected from further suffering at the hands of the state and whilst I am satisfied that there are certain structural checks and balances I remain deeply sceptical as to the need for this provision, which I view as further political exploitation of a very vulnerable constituency – all this for the tenuous objective of "closure". The entire context of the debate is so contaminated by the politics of hate that I believe it is almost impossible to gain a rational assessment of what the positive outcomes are for victim witnesses. It seems to me that by complying with this demand the state hopes to be in a position to divest itself of further responsibility having surrendered any remnants of political courage in their dealings with the pro-punishment victims' lobby.

It was not until victims' families were allowed to witness executions that the above measures were implemented despite the fact that the families of the condemned have been witnessing executions for decades. Thankfully this omission has now been addressed. The pastoral responsibility for these families has been delegated to the Prison Chaplains' department which attempts to provide a similar service to that provided to the victim witnesses. It could be argued that the experiences of these "secondary victims" at the hands of the criminal justice system equals, perhaps exceeds, the suffering of the victim's family. I say exceed because their experience is aggravated by a largely unsympathetic legal and penal system as compared to the experience of the family of the victim.

Another project overseen by the Victim Services Division is the Victim Offender Mediation / Dialogue (VOM/D) whose objectives are as follows:[1]

- To provide victims of violent crime with the opportunity to have a structured face-to-face meeting with "their" offenders in a secure, safe environment, in order to facilitate a healing recovery process.

- To provide victims with the opportunity for personal insight, empowerment, and structure for their grieving and healing.

- For offenders to express remorse, admit guilt and take responsibility for the full impact of their behaviour upon the victims, their families and their communities.

---

1. Victim Offender Mediation / Dialogue, Texas Department of Criminal Justice, Victim Services Division 7800 Shoal Creek Blvd., Suite 230-S, Austin, Texas 78757. Tel: +1 (512) 406 5620.

To provide a process for developing mutual agreements, insights or projects that could serve to benefit other victims and offenders in similar circumstances; such as mutual commitment to crime prevention, an assurance of personal safety, victim advocacy, service to/within the community, criminal justice reform, victim impact panels.

Figures for January 1998 showed that, so far, some 328 victims had requested to meet with their offenders, 11 have been completed with a further 60 under review. Of the 328 cases, murderers account for 168 of whom 33 are on death row. On their own initiative 43 offenders have sought mediation through the VOM/D programme. This is a recent initiative so any evaluation of its effectiveness is limited though reports indicate room for optimism, with benefits for both victims/victims' families and for offenders. The important principle to be remembered here is that this scheme is essentially for the victims unlike some earlier projects which brought together victims with their offenders where victims were clearly being "used" as part of the offender's therapy programme. Quite how the principles of this project which are about healing and conciliation, perhaps even forgiveness and reconciliation, lie with the somewhat vengeful aims of the execution witness programme is difficult to imagine. Does the therapeutic environment of the former lead to "closure" more effectively and for greater duration than the medieval approach of the latter where instant but transient benefits are on offer? I look forward to seeing an independent evaluation of the benefits of both schemes.

Conclusions

The intellectual argument about the purpose and the effect of the death penalty has long been favourable to those opposed to capital punishment. The moral argument so far as international human rights treaties and the mainstream religious groups, save Islam and the Mormon Church, is also on the side of the abolitionist. The emotional argument however, about the needs and rights of victims and their families and friends is definitely with the pro-punishment lobby. The emotional appeal is very compelling and even more compelling when it appears, even to neutral observers that abolitionists and other penal reform groups are only concerned about the needs and rights of offenders. It is for this reason that reform organisations such as Amnesty International (UK), Hands off Cain (Italy), the National Coalition for the Abolition of the Death Penalty (USA) and the Howard League for Penal Reform (UK), amongst others, need to review their aims and objectives. Positive statements need to be made reflecting concern for the needs and rights of crime victims. As far as I can establish Amnesty International refers only once to victims in its constitution and does so in the paragraph illustrating its independence: "Amnesty International is independent of any government, political persuasion or religious creed. It does not support or oppose any government or political system, nor does it support or oppose the views of victims whose rights it seeks to protect. It is concerned solely with the impartial protection of human rights." The victims it refers to are those who suffer at the hands of the state in circumstances such as torture – not crime victims. As for Hands off Cain, the author, a founding member of that organisation, (which has done much this past five years to successfully promote the abolitionist agenda) remembers being a lone advocate for the inclusion of explicit statements about concern for homicide victims and their families and friends. Sadly his appeals went unheeded. The Howard League, on whose council I sit, have recently reaffirmed their commitment to the needs of crime victims which is entirely compatible with their overarching objective to create a civilised, humane and effective penal system (see footnote 2, p. 47).

There is little doubt that that the pro-punishment victim movement attracts significant public and political support in the United States across party lines, contrasted with the United Kingdom where the public support for punishment is arguably as strong as in the United States but crucially without the same support from mainstream political and victims' groups. Death penalty abolitionists have a steep hill to climb if they hope to influence this emotionally charged debate and the ground they have to make up is largely of their own creation – crucial to their future strategy has to be an explicit recognition of the needs and rights of victims. I am not suggesting a cynical adoption of a victim-friendly strategy but the acceptance that homicide victims and those that survive them have inherent rights and that these should be recognised. The failure to do so has driven many moderate, perhaps anti-death penalty victims' families, reluctantly into the arms of the pro-lobby who can and do offer succour and "solutions" to the hurt, anger and frustration experienced by such families. The menu of "rights" referred to earlier represent the incline of the hill that has to be climbed and could form the basis for discussion – had the debate been engaged earlier then I suspect that many of the items would not be on the menu.

This very full menu of rights that the bereaved have sought and won is an indication of how such families and friends can and have influenced the very philosophy that the state pursues in capital cases. For example, two issues that have always been on the periphery of this debate, mode of execution and live broadcasts of executions, are beginning to gain more attention from the "populist" victim lobby and First Amendment challenges are again being made by media groups. The demands are to allow media witnesses to view the entire execution process and to permit recorded and/or live broadcasts.

Constitutional issues aside, these proposals have divided the abolitionist community as some believe that live broadcasts will aid the abolitionist agenda while others view the prospect as pandering to gratuitous needs which have no social utility. The mode of execution debate goes to the heart of the modern purpose of the death penalty – retribution. The move towards the more sanitised and clinical lethal injection represents an interesting dilemma; on the one hand it is an attempt to make the execution process more civilised and therefore more acceptable, whilst on the other it represents a dilution of the retributive justification. Those states that maintain the electric chair do so because they believe the process has to appear to be painful but not that painful as to violate the Eighth Amendment to the United States' Constitution.

Reform groups have to counter the advances made and it is not enough for them to rely on the intellectual and academic evidence that the death penalty serves no useful purpose and that it is a vehicle for a multitude of abuses of due process and human rights. Whilst all this is correct it fails to address the needs of even the moderate victim lobby and it is this failure historically that has lead to the birth of the angry, frustrated and pro-punishment victims' groups in the United States. The dominant debate on victims' needs and rights is provided by those victims' groups that focus on influencing penal policy rather than, and some would say, at the expense of the more traditional needs of crime victims – the crime victim movement has become a political movement typified by the vocabulary, rhetoric and aggressive tactics of the Pro-Life movement.

Abolition of the death penalty and penal reform in general is not to be gained at the expense of the inherent needs and rights of crime victims. The simple analysis provided by some politicians that money spent on offenders is money denied to victim services is a fallacy. Victims' needs and rights should not be met at the expense of humane, effective and proportional responses to offenders and their needs should not be confused with or influence the treatment of offenders.

4. The efforts of the Parliamentary Assembly of the Council of Europe

Renate Wohlwend, member of the Liechtenstein delegation to the Parliamentary Assembly of the Council of Europe

---

Of all the struggles for the development of human rights and for the respect of human dignity, the one to abolish the death penalty seems the hardest to win.

The Parliamentary Assembly has always taken a very firm position on the issue of the abolition of capital punishment. It considers that the death penalty has no legitimate place in the penal systems of modern civilised societies, and that its application may well be compared with torture and be seen as inhuman and degrading punishment within the meaning of Article 3 of the European Convention on Human Rights, and thus as a violation of the most fundamental right, that to life itself. The Assembly believes that the imposition of the death penalty has proved ineffective as a deterrent, and owing to the possible fallibility of human justice, also tragic through the execution of innocent people.

Consequently, the willingness to institute an immediate moratorium on executions and to abolish the death penalty in the long-term has become, since 1994, a precondition for accession to the Council of Europe.

As a result of the Assembly's position, Europe has become *de facto* a death-penalty-free zone, with all of the Council of Europe's forty-one member states either having abolished the death penalty, or having instituted a moratorium on executions.

This was not easy to achieve, and often needed repeated prodding by the Assembly. However, the momentum towards the abolition of the death penalty in Europe is growing ever more rapidly; Georgia has acceded as the forty-first member state of the Council of Europe, free of the death penalty.

When did the Parliamentary Assembly start its activities in that matter?

It was in 1973 when a motion for a resolution[1] on the abolition of capital punishment was presented by Miss Bergegren and others, which was referred back to the Committee on Legal Affairs. There were long-lasting discussions within the committee in 1974 and 1975 and the then appointed rapporteur had to revise his report, but when in January 1976 the Legal Affairs Committee decided to defer the question, Mr Lidgard resigned as rapporteur. It was not until the beginning of 1979 that the committee decided to take up the question again and to appoint another rapporteur who was Mr Lidbom.

Thanks to his report[2] together with the resolution[3] and recommendation[4] passed by the Parliamentary Assembly on 22 April 1980 the Council of Europe achieved Protocol No.6 to the Convention for the Protection of Human Rights and Fundamental Freedoms concerning the Abolition of the Death Penalty, drawn up by the Steering Committee on Human Rights and adopted by the Committee of Ministers. The protocol was opened for signature by the member states of the Council of Europe on 28 April 1983. Twelve of then twenty-one member states signed it on this date: Austria, Belgium, Denmark, France, Germany, Luxembourg, Netherlands, Norway, Portugal, Spain, Sweden and Switzerland. The entry into force on 1 March 1985 was achieved with the essential five ratifications of Austria, Denmark, Luxembourg, Spain and Sweden.

Protocol No. 6 is the first agreement under international law containing the legal obligation of the parties to abolish the death penalty.

To date thirty of the forty-one members of the Council of Europe have ratified Protocol No.6: Andorra (1996), Austria (1984), Belgium (1998), Croatia (1997), Czech Republic (1993), Denmark (1985), Estonia (1998), Finland (1990), France (1986), Germany (1989), Greece (1998), Hungary (1992), Iceland (1987), Ireland (1994), Italy (1989), Liechtenstein (1990), Luxembourg (1985), Malta (1991), Moldova (1997), Netherlands (1986), Norway (1988), Portugal (1986), Romania (1994), San Marino (1989), Slovakia (1993), Slovenia (1994), Spain (1985), Sweden (1985), Switzerland (1987), and "the former Yugoslav Republic of Macedonia" (1997); only five member states are not signatories of the Protocol, namely Albania, Bulgaria, Cyprus, Poland and Turkey. But it is to be said that Bulgaria and Poland have abolished the death penalty in their legislation.

---

1. See Parliamentary Assembly Document 3297 (1973).
2. See Parliamentary Assembly Document 4509 (1980).
3. See Parliamentary Assembly Resolution 727 (1980).
4. See Parliamentary Assembly Recommendation 891 (1980).

Others have signed but not yet ratified Protocol No. 6: Latvia, Lithuania, the Russian Federation, Ukraine and the United Kingdom.

Lithuania signed Protocol No. 6 on 18 January 1999 and the United Kingdom signed on 27 January 1999, which – from the Assembly's point of view might be seen as the latest events in that matter.

The rapporteur received good news on 12 February 1999 by the announce-ment of Mr Anatoly Pristavkin, head of the Russian Presidential Pardons Commission, that all prisoners sentenced to the death penalty would have their sentences commuted to terms of imprisonment by June 1999.

Finally, on 18 February 1999, the Parliament of Cyprus unanimously voted for the abolition of the death penalty under domestic law.

The chronology of reports debated in several sittings of the Parliamentary Assembly is as follows.

In autumn 1994 Mr Hans Göran Franck submitted his report[1] on the aboli-tion of capital punishment, on the basis of which on 4 October 1994 the Parliamentary Assembly adopted Resolution 1044 (1994) and Recommendation 1246 (1994). The rapporteur had rightly discerned a strong abolitionist current in member states of the Council of Europe at the time. The Assembly followed his lead in recommending that the Committee of Ministers draw up an additional protocol to the European Convention on Human Rights (ECHR), abolishing the death penalty both in peace and wartime, and obliging the signatories not to reintroduce it under any cir-cumstances. The Assembly also recommended the setting-up of a control mechanism under the Secretary General and the organisation of a confer-ence on the abolition of the death penalty to take place in 1995.

Possibly, even more importantly, the Assembly decided that the willingness to sign and ratify Protocol No. 6 to the ECHR was to be a prerequisite for membership of the Council of Europe. Accordingly, since October 1994 all applicant states had to enter into commitments vis-à-vis the Assembly dur-ing the accession procedure to sign and ratify that protocol within a given period. States which were still executing prisoners condemned to death were furthermore obliged to introduce moratoria on executions with effect from the day of accession to the Council of Europe.

The great success in the aftermath of that debate was that Belgium, Italy, Moldova and Spain abolished the death penalty completely, but unfortu-nately other countries gave no heed to the Assembly's call and paid no respect to their commitments in this matter.

---

1. See Parliamentary Assembly Document 7154 (1994).

Having discovered that executions were still carried out in Latvia, Russia and Ukraine, and being convinced that some of the prisoners on death row could still be saved from certain death by timely Council of Europe intervention, the Committee on Legal Affairs and Human Rights asked that a debate be held under the emergency procedure to follow up on Mr Franck's 1994 report. The current author submitted a report[1] and the Assembly's debate took place on 28 June 1996. In my report I described the positive and negative developments between October 1994 and June 1996. Further, I dealt with the futility of capital punishment. Many people are in favour of retaining the death penalty because they believe that this will bring down the crime rate. This "deterrence" argument is simply wrong. A survey of research findings on the relation between the death penalty and homicide rates, conducted by the United Nations in 1988, concluded that "this research has failed to provide scientific proof that executions have a greater deterrent effect than life imprisonment. Such proof is unlikely to be forthcoming. The evidence as a whole still gives no positive support to the deterrent hypothesis."

The experience of abolitionist states should be convincing proof in and of itself. For example, the homicide rate in Canada has continued to fall since the abolition of the death penalty for murder in 1976, while the neighbouring United States, which resumed the use of capital punishment in 1977, has seen a continuing rise in the rate of violent crimes, including murder. No abolitionist country experienced a sudden and serious change in the curve of crime following the abolition of the death penalty; on the contrary, since executions brutalise society, the effect of abolition has on the whole been positive.

However, the strongest possible argument is probably the risk of executing the innocent.

According to an article (*Die Welt*, 11 November 1998) so many judicial errors occur in the United States that the "survivors of death row" have meetings. For instance in Chicago, organised by the North-Western University, twenty-nine people met in order to discuss their fate. Too many people are wrongly convicted. People who have been killed legally by the state can never be brought back to life, even if their innocence is later proven. Between 1976 and 1997 seventy-four innocent men and women were able to escape their execution.

If this can happen in the United States, with its history of democracy and rule of law, how much higher must be the risk of executing the innocent in

---

1. See Parliamentary Assembly Document 7589 (1996).

countries with criminal justice systems that have only just come out of the totalitarian yoke and are still in need of reform?

Another reason sometimes given for retaining the death penalty is that public opinion demands it. Polls often show considerable support for capital punishment, especially in times of rising crime rates, or following a particularly heinous or violent crime. But history and research show that the population's attitude to the death penalty changes with more knowledge of the facts, and with the abolitionist experience.

Whilst most of the paragraphs in the resolution[1] and in the recommendation[2] resulting from the Assembly's debate of June 1996 recalled previous decisions, an important step forward, supported by the Assembly, was contained in the respective order,[3] namely to instruct the Committee on Legal Affairs and Human Rights to organise one or two seminars on the abolition of the death penalty in Europe, and to report back on developments in due course.

The Assembly has been trying to help those countries which would like to abolish capital punishment or have committed themselves to do so. An example is the Seminar on the Abolition of the Death Penalty organised by the Committee on Legal Affairs and Human Rights in co-operation with the Ukrainian Ministry of Justice, which took place in Kyiv at the end of November 1996; its aim was to press ahead despite the opposition from public opinion, key ministries or senior officials. Over a hundred participants, most of them from central and eastern European countries, were present in the seminar. The debates were open to the press, and they really offered the opportunity for the Ministers for Justice, the Ministers of the Interior and the Attorney Generals, chairs of parliamentary legal committees, as well as for representatives from NGOs and international experts, to discuss such themes as capital punishment and human rights, the incidence of the death penalty relating to the crime rate and the influence of public opinion.

On the occasion of that seminar members of the Committee on Legal Affairs and Human Rights got to know from Mr Anatoly Pristavkin, Chairman of the Russian Presidential Pardons Commission, as well as from Mr Serhiy Holovatiy, then Minister for Justice in Ukraine, that death sentences were still being carried out, that the deputies were in principle powerless compared with their ministers, and that their governments were behaving as though they had never welcomed the moratorium and accepted it voluntarily.

1. See Parliamentary Assembly Resolution 1097 (1996).
2. See Parliamentary Assembly Recommendation 1302 (1996).
3. See Parliamentary Assembly Order No. 525 (1996).

Further, the Parliamentary Assembly received reliable information that in the first half year of 1996, numerous executions of the death penalty were carried out in Russia.

Therefore, on 29 January 1997, the Parliamentary Assembly held another emergency debate on the reports concerning the honouring of the commitments entered into by Ukraine[1] and Russia[2], upon accession to the Council of Europe, to put into place a moratorium on the executions of death sentences. In Resolution 1112 (1997), the Assembly condemned Ukraine for having violated her commitment to put into place a moratorium on executions, and deplored the eighty-nine executions that had already taken place in the first half year of 1996. It declared itself particularly shocked by the information that executions in Ukraine were shrouded in secrecy, with apparently not even the families of the prisoners being informed, and that the executed were reportedly buried in unmarked graves. The Assembly warned the Ukrainian authorities that "it will take all necessary steps to ensure compliance with commitments entered into", including, if necessary, the non-ratification of the credentials of the Ukrainian parliamentary delegation at its next part-session.

The same warning was given to the Russian authorities, in Resolution 1111 (1997). After that, Russia has not executed anybody since August 1996. However, there are hundreds of people on death row.

Concerning Ukraine, at the end of summer 1997 news of secret executions in 1997 started to leak out. Some NGOs were concerned that they had no news from certain death-row prisoners for a long time making them fear that they had been executed. Even more worrying, the former Minister for Justice, Mr Holovatiy, declared to the press, that thirteen executions had taken place in the first half of 1997, even naming the precise regions where they had been carried out. Two Deputy Ministers for Justice confirmed this information to deputies of the Verkhovna Rada (the parliament) and to NGO activists in August 1997 in writing. However, when these letters were made available to the public, an international outcry followed, in the wake of which the Deputy Ministers retracted their statements and blamed the "false" information on a statistical error. Confusion reigned until the beginning of October 1997 when the President of Ukraine informed the President of the Assembly during the second summit of the Council of Europe that he had not refused mercy to any death-row inmate since 29 November 1996. However, he also stated that the last execution in his country took place in March 1997. Despite attempts by both the Assembly President and the

---

1. See Parliamentary Assembly Document 7745 (1997).
2. See Parliamentary Assembly Document 7746 (1997).

Secretary General to obtain more precise official information on this matter, no further light was shed by officials on the alleged breaking of the moratorium.

Thus, the Committee on Legal Affairs and Human Rights instructed its rapporteur to go on a fact-finding mission to Ukraine. This mission took place from 5 to 7 November 1997, I was accompanied by Mrs Tanja Kleinsorge. The programme was very well-organised by the Ukrainian authorities and I was able to meet the Minister for Justice, the Minister of the Interior, the Prosecutor General and the Ukrainian parliamentary delegation. I was also allowed to visit three pre-trial detention centres in different parts of the country and to meet death-row inmates whom I had asked to see in two of these prisons. Senior officials confirmed that a *de facto* moratorium on executions was in place since 11 March 1997.

There shall follow some explanations of the procedure as to how death sentences are confirmed and carried out in Ukraine, and some impressions of the conditions on death row.

The court of first instance that can hand down sentences in Ukraine is the regional (*oblast*) court. According to information received even from death-row prisoners, lawyers are usually present during the trials at regional court level, although they are not always present during the first days of police custody, interrogation and investigation. Few prisoners can, however, afford the services of a lawyer to help them draw up an appeal to the Supreme Court (the court of second instance in death penalty cases), so most prisoners seem to draw up their appeals to the Supreme Court themselves.

If the Supreme Court confirms the death sentence (which it does in most cases), the inmate has five days in which to appeal to the President for mercy. If the prisoner himself does not draw up an appeal for mercy, the prison governor is obliged to do that on his behalf. The President, advised by a special pardons commission, has the right to pardon the death-row inmates and commute their sentences; most often to twenty years' imprisonment, life imprisonment not being foreseen by Ukraine's criminal justice system.

If the President refuses to pardon the prisoner, he informs the Supreme Court of this decision, which in turn instructs the Ministry of the Interior to carry out the death sentence. In practice, a special unit of the Ministry of the Interior (called the *convoi*) will arrive at the pre-trial detention centre where the prisoner is held. The prison governor is then obliged to turn over the inmate to the *convoi* (without prior notification of either the governor or the inmate). The inmate is then transferred to an unknown destination where he is shot dead.

The Ministry of the Interior then informs the Supreme Court in writing that the sentence has been carried out. It has five days to do so. The Supreme Court sends back the whole file to the (regional) court of first instance, which has the task of informing the relatives of the inmate of the execution within ten days of receipt of the file. The regional courts draw up statistics bi-annually on executions, which are sent to the Ministry of Justice, the Supreme Court and possibly, also to the Prosecutor General.

The whole procedure is shrouded in secrecy. The State Committee on Secrets, chaired by the Deputy Minister of the Interior, declared the following data to be state secrets: information on management, conditions and supervision of places of imprisonment, including corrective medical institutions and other punitive institutions where sentenced persons work, and information regarding executions of capital punishment, the organisation of the execution and burial, the place of execution, the place of burial and the people who have carried out the execution. In conformity with these rules, relatives of executed prisoners are not informed where their relatives are buried, which is an affront to human dignity. Even prison governors receive their information on executions – including on the moratorium currently in force – from the media.

Conditions on death row which I saw in three pre-trial detention centres, namely Donetsk No. 1, Simferopol and Khmelnitsky, varied slightly. The internal regulations of the Ministry of the Interior mandate the following:

- death-row inmates must wear special clothing (black), they may not leave their cells, except to have a shower;
- they are not allowed to walk in the corridors or in the courtyards.
- death-row inmates may be kept in single or double cells;
- death-row inmates are not allowed to communicate with other inmates except their cell-mate, if they have one;
- death-row inmates are permitted one short visit a month by no more than two relatives. There is no limit to the amount of letters that can be written or received, but these are censored.

In November 1997 there were thirty-six death-row inmates in pre-trial detention centre Donetsk No. 1. Two of these were kept in single cells, the rest in double cells. The cell I saw was a double cell, extremely small, with one bunk-bed, one other bed, one (open) toilet, one washbasin with cold water and one light which was left on day and night. There was some fresh air through a ventilation system, but no daylight, and practically no room to move around. Inmates are allowed to shower, once every ten days, and read books from the prison library. They are woken at 5 a.m. and given three meals a day through the hatch. They are constantly watched through a peephole in the door, allowing them not a minute's privacy. The inmate I spoke to had lived in these conditions since 19 November 1992.

There were twenty-eight death-row inmates in Simferopol pre-trial detention centre, all kept in double cells. I saw one of those, which was of acceptable size, but with not a single piece of furniture. There were only three concrete platforms in the concrete floor that served as beds, and a toilet with cold water flowing into it constantly instead of a washbasin. There was a shuttered window through which fresh air could get through, and a light which was on day and night. Inmates were allowed to a shower once every five days, and to read books, newspapers and magazines of their choice. Security seemed a little less tight.

In Khmelnitzky there were six death-row inmates, all of whom were kept in single cells. The empty cell I saw was of acceptable size, had two bunk beds and was adequately furnished, it had a wooden floor, there was an open toilet and a washbasin. There was a shuttered window through which some fresh air filtered, but no daylight. Inmates, here, are allowed a shower once a week, and may read books, newspapers and magazines.

Three inmates who had wished to meet with a representative of the Council of Europe declined, at short notice, to meet with me. One can only assume there must have been some pressure put on them.

Shocked to find that thirteen executions had taken place in Ukraine and equally shocked by the secrecy surrounding the death penalty and executions in the country, as well as by the living conditions of death-row inmates I wrote another report[1] and suggested to the Committee on Legal Affairs and Human Rights that a debate should be held during the January 1998 part-session.

After a realistic, but also emotional debate on 27 January 1998 Resolution 1145 (1998) was adopted by the Assembly in which it recalled its Opinion No. 190 (1995) on the application by Ukraine for membership of the Council of Europe which noted that she committed herself to "put into place, with immediate effect from the day of accession, a moratorium on executions". So, the Assembly demanded – once again – that no more executions be carried out under any circumstances whatsoever. It demanded that the secrecy surrounding executions be lifted without further delay, and that a list of all those who have been under sentence of death, and their ultimate fate, since the accession to the Council of Europe on 9 November 1995 be made public.

---

1. See Parliamentary Assembly Document 7974 (1997).

The Assembly also demanded that the death penalty be abolished by parliament as soon as a new parliament has been elected and that the President pardon all current death-row inmates. Further, it insisted that all death-row inmates be allowed one hour's exercise outside, in fresh air, per day. Lights that can be turned down at night should be installed in death-row cells; where possible, daylight should be allowed into the cells as well as fresh air.

With Order No. 538 (1998) the Assembly instructed the Committee on Legal Affairs and Human Rights to evaluate the proof, to be furnished by the Ukrainian authorities, that a moratorium on executions has been established.

Since then, the Ukrainian authorities and parliament have carried out both undertakings. By her letter dated 31 March 1998 the Minister for Justice confirmed vis-à-vis the President of the Assembly that her ministry had abolished the secrecy rules from data concerning execution of capital punishment, according to instructions given by the President and the Prime Minister of Ukraine. In September the parliament passed the first reading of the new Criminal Code abolishing the death penalty.

On 27 January 1999 the Assembly debated a report of the Committee on Legal Affairs and Human Rights on the honouring of obligations and commitments by member states of the Council of Europe. Thereby the Parliamentary Assembly passed Resolution 1179 (1999) and resolved Recommendation 1395 (1999) in which it made reference to previous debates.

The Assembly took a decision that, should substantial progress in the honouring of certain commitments (including ratification of Protocol No. 6) not be taken by the opening of 1 June 1999 part-session, it shall proceed to the annulment of the credentials of the Ukrainian parliamentary delegation in accordance with Rule 6 of its Rules of Procedure, until these commitments have been fully complied with. Further, it recommends that the Committee of Ministers proceed to suspend Ukraine from its right of representation, in conformity with Article 8 of the Statute of the Council of Europe.

The death penalty in observer states of the Council of Europe

During the debates held in the Assembly on the abolition of the death penalty, some speakers made reference to the United States of America. Many American states still have capital punishment on their statute books, and some states are executing an ever-increasing number of prisoners. The speakers felt that it was unfair that the Assembly harried some Council of Europe member states such as Russia, Ukraine and the Baltic states to abolish the death penalty, while the United States was not penalised although it was an observer state. Convinced of the necessity to deal with the abolition of the death penalty in observer states such as the United States I, together with twenty-eight colleagues representing a wide range of countries and political groups, tabled a motion for a resolution on 5 February 1998 on the abolition of the death penalty in the United States of America. The motion was referred to the Committee on Legal Affairs and Human Rights for report, which appointed me rapporteur on 23 March 1998.

According to Statutory Resolution (93) 26 on observer status:

> "Any state willing to accept the principles of democracy, the rule of law and the enjoyment by all persons within its jurisdiction of human rights and fundamental freedoms, ... may be granted ... observer status with the Organisation."

Observer status with the Council of Europe has been granted to Canada, Japan and the United States. Of these three countries Japan and the United States still apply the death penalty. Both of these states were addressed in my Introductory Memorandum, since there should be no double standards with regard to observer states in relation to member states of the Council of Europe.

Observer states must be willing to accept the enjoyment by all persons within their jurisdiction of human rights and fundamental freedoms. While the European Convention on Human Rights (ECHR) still allows the application of the death penalty, "in the execution of a sentence of a court following his conviction of a crime for which this penalty is provided by law", it does not permit torture, inhuman or degrading treatment or punishment.

As described above, subsequent texts in the Council of Europe have upheld the right to life more strictly: The Protocol No. 6 of the ECHR abolishes the death penalty, and the case-law of the European Court of Human Rights (especially the landmark *Soering* case) finds the "death-row phenomenon" to be inhuman and degrading treatment. The Assembly has gone even further, classifying the application of the death penalty itself as inhuman and degrading punishment, and thus a violation of the most fundamental human right, that to life itself. Under these circumstances, the Assembly must consider observer states which still apply the death penalty to be violating human rights, and therefore in contravention of Statutory Resolution (93) 26 on observer status.

It would not be my intention to put into question the observer status of Japan or the United States but it is to be hoped that, through contact and co-operation with both of these countries, they may be persuaded to put into place a moratorium on executions. Some people will say that this is an unrealistic goal – but then, was it not unrealistic for the late Hans Göran Franck in 1994 to dream of a death-penalty-free Europe, a goal that has now been achieved?

The aim of the rapporteur is to bring a report on that matter to the Committee of Legal Affairs and Human Rights as soon as possible and then to have an Assembly debate in the January part-session 2000, at the latest.

Miscellaneous

In late 1998 a Russian female democratic politician was murdered and the criminal procedure against a multiple murderer in Ukraine was opened; in that connection several high-ranking politicians and officials in both Russia and Ukraine indicated that capital punishment should be imposed again in both countries. The Committee on Legal Affairs and Human Rights, meeting in Paris, was extremely concerned by such statements and arranged a press release on 8 December 1998 in order to remind Ukraine and Russia of their commitments entered into when acceding to the Council of Europe in 9 November 1995 and 28 February 1996 respectively.

How did and does Liechtenstein deal with the death penalty? The last execution in Liechtenstein took place in 1785. But, it has been only ten years (1 January 1989) since the death penalty was struck off the Penal Code. Since then the maximum punishment has been life imprisonment which is imposed for murder and genocide. According to the Liechtenstein Constitution the prince has the prerogative of remitting, mitigating or commuting sentences which have been legally pronounced.

The Liechtenstein Constitution does not contain any provision with respect to capital punishment. However, according to the prevailing doctrine, Protocol No. 6 to the ECHR which Liechtenstein ratified on 15 November 1990, and the Second Optional Protocol to the International Covenant on Civil and Political Rights aiming at the abolition of the death penalty, to which Liechtenstein acceded on 10 December 1998, have at least the status of law. Upon its accession to the Second Optional Protocol Liechtenstein did not make any reservation as to the application of the death penalty in time of war.

Under the law on mutual assistance in criminal matters of 11 November 1992 the government, when examining a decision for extradition, has to make sure that existing obligations of the principality of Liechtenstein under international law have duly been taken into account. Among these obligations under international law is the provision of the European Convention on Extradition which stipulates that extradition may be refused if the offence for which extradition is requested is punishable by death under the law of the requesting party.

The conviction that the abolition of the death penalty contributes to the progressive development of human rights is also the basis of the attitude of Liechtenstein towards this matter in international bodies. Thus, Liechtenstein was, for instance, a co-sponsor of Resolution 1997/12 and Resolution 1998/8 of the United Nations Commission on Human Rights which aim at abolishing the death penalty worldwide.

In some reports presented to the Assembly from the beginning, and in some speeches of parliamentarians at the accompanying debates, the following sentence was very often quoted: "In the United Europe of tomorrow ... the formal abolition of capital punishment should be the first article of the European Code for which we all hope."[1]

We are already very near the United Europe of tomorrow; 1999 Europe has become *de facto* a death penalty-free zone, with all the Council of Europe's forty-one member states either having abolished the death penalty, or having instituted a moratorium on executions.

Therefore, the members of the Parliamentary Assembly and the Assembly as such will not cease their struggle before they reach their goal, the *de jure* abolition of the death penalty.

---

1. Albert Camus (Calmann-Lévy, 1978). "Réflexions sur la guillotine" (in Arthur Koestler and Albert Camus: *Réflexions sur la peine capitale*, Paris, p. 176.

5. PROTOCOL NO. 6 TO THE EUROPEAN CONVENTION ON HUMAN RIGHTS

Hans Christian Krüger, Deputy Secretary General of the Council of Europe

---

This chapter presents a brief history of Protocol No. 6 to the European Convention on Human Rights and comments on its place in the framework of the human rights protection and political activities of the Council of Europe.

Three years after the second world war, leading politicians gathered in The Hague to launch a project of European reconciliation and reunification. The declaration they adopted gave rise to the birth of the Council of Europe on 5 May 1949, when its statute was signed by ten countries.

In what must be considered record time for international treaty making, the European Convention on Human Rights was adopted on 4 November 1950, that is, only sixteen months later. The Convention, which entered into force on 3 September 1953, is a catalogue of fundamental rights and freedoms, subject to the control of the European Court of Human Rights and the system of collective enforcement through the Committee of Ministers of the Council of Europe.[1]

Article 2, paragraph 1, of the European Convention on Human Rights specifies that everyone's life shall be protected by law and that no one shall be deprived of his life intentionally, save in the execution of a sentence of a court following his conviction of a crime for which this penalty is provided by law.

The Convention thus reserves the right of a state to impose capital punishment on condition that this punishment was foreseen in its national legislation and subsequently confirmed by a court of law.

---

1. Protocol No. 11 to the ECHR establishes the single Court. See also Article 46.2 of the ECHR, as amended by Protocol No. 11.

But barely four years after the entry into force of the Convention, there was a move at expert level in the Council of Europe to "study the problems of capital punishment in Europe". For a long time, this work did not yield results and it was only towards the end of the 1970s – following proposals from the Parliamentary Assembly of the Council of Europe – that the Committee of Ministers was invited to consider capital punishment as "inhuman" and to elaborate an additional protocol abolishing this punishment for crimes committed in times of peace.[1]

Similar proposals were also made by conferences of Ministers for Justice of the Council of Europe which considered that Article 2 of the Convention no longer reflected public opinion in Europe.

As a result, the Committee of Ministers, in 1982, mandated its Steering Committee for Human Rights to "prepare a draft additional protocol to the European Convention on Human Rights abolishing the death penalty in peace time". The text was prepared in approximately one year and was opened for signature on 28 April 1983.[2]

Protocol No. 6 of the European Convention on Human Rights entered into force on 1 March 1985, following the fifth ratification by a member state of the Council of Europe. (The full text of this protocol is reproduced in Appendix I.)

The protocol includes features which are less common in international legal instruments.[3]

The wording of Article 1 is unique in the sense that it does not oblige states to act through the introduction of national legislation. Instead, it directly prohibits capital punishment. Secondly, states are not allowed to make reservations when ratifying the protocol.[4] Thirdly, the protection against capital punishment under Protocol No. 6 is unconditional and cannot be suspended by Article 15 of the Convention, which otherwise allows contracting parties "in times of war or other public emergency threatening the life of the nation" to take "measures derogating from its obligations – to the extent strictly required by the exigencies of the situation".[5]

---

1. See Parliamentary Assembly Resolution 727 (1980) and Recommendation 891 (1980).
2. See 1983 Explanatory Report on Protocol No. 6 to the Convention for the Protection of Human Rights and Fundamental Freedoms concerning the abolition of the death penalty (No. 114). Council of Europe Publishing, ISBN-92-871-0216-3.
3. For further detailed comments, see Pettiti, Decaux and Imbert, "La Convention européenne des droits de l'homme" (1955), *Economica*; pp. 1067 et seq.
4. That is other than interpretative reservations, see Article 64 of the ECHR (i.e. Article 57 as amended by Protocol No. 11) and Article 4, Protocol No. 6 to the ECHR.
5. Article 3, Protocol No. 6 to the ECHR.

Finally, it should be mentioned that Protocol No. 6 is subject to the same formal conditions of denunciation as other articles of and protocols to the Convention, that is, only after the expiry of five years from the date on which it became a party to it and after six months' notice to the Secretary General of the Council of Europe.[1]

The case-law of Protocol No. 6 is the subject of Chapter 6 in this publication. Suffice it to say here that the Protocol has been invoked to refuse requests for extradition from a Council of Europe member state to third countries in which capital punishment still exists.[2]

The right to life is certainly among the most fundamental of human rights. It is protected also in other international human rights treaties, such as Article 3 of the Universal Declaration on Human Rights, Article 6 of the International Covenant on Civil and Political Rights and Article 4 of the African Charter on Human and Peoples' Rights.

But it is clear from the foregoing that neither Article 2 of the ECHR, nor Protocol No. 6, provide an unconditional protection from execution since it is still authorised "in time of war or in imminent threat of war". Nor do these texts guarantee a certain quality of life. The main purpose is to protect the individual against arbitrary execution.

The fall of the Berlin Wall fundamentally changed the European political landscape. After forty years as a mainly western European organisation, the Council of Europe was finally able to play the pan-European role foreseen by its founding fathers and to fulfil the very *raison d'être* of the Organisation: the extension of democratic pluralism, human rights and the pre-eminence of law in a re-united Europe without dividing lines in which almost 800 million people share the same values.

The first summit of the Council of Europe (Vienna, 1993) acknowledged the Organisation as being the pre-eminent European political institution with a mission to include all democracies of Europe on an equal footing. The Vienna Summit also defined the political criteria for accession to the Council of Europe which presuppose that applicant states have brought their institutions and legal systems into line with the basic principles of democracy, the rule of law and respect for human rights; that the people's representatives have been chosen by means of free and fair elections, based upon universal suffrage and the freedom of expression, in particular of the media; that there is proper protection of national minorities and observance of international

---

1. Article 65 of the ECHR.
2. Case of *Soering* (7 July 1989, judgment A No. 161, paragraph 82).

law and furthermore an undertaking to sign and ratify the Convention on Human Rights and an acceptance of the Convention's supervisory machinery. Finally, the Vienna Summit also confirmed the responsibility of the Council of Europe in ensuring compliance with the commitments accepted by all member states.

What are these commitments? In the Council of Europe context we speak of three types of commitments. Looking at these in the order in which the applicant states encounter them, the first category is individualised commitments, entered into with varying degrees of explicitness, normally during the negotiations on accession to the Organisation, for example to sign and ratify a specific convention within a certain time limit. These commitments are incorporated in the opinions by which the Assembly has given its support for the admission of new members.

The second category is commitments made in the course of member states' participation in Council of Europe activities, again often in the form of accepting conventions whose ratification entail legal obligations to comply with their basic provisions and to participate in their supervisory machinery where such exists.

The third and most obvious category covers commitments which follow from the Council of Europe's statute, comprising principles which all members accept, namely the rule of law and the enjoyment by all persons within member states' jurisdiction of human and fundamental freedoms. Moreover, member states reaffirm their attachment to genuine democracy which in itself is based on the foregoing values.

In the last decade, the Council of Europe has doubled its membership from twenty to forty-one states. In recent years, three states have also been granted observer status (Canada, United States and Japan). On the threshold of the next millennium the enlargement of the Council of Europe is almost completed. The challenge now is to ensure – in line with the Vienna Summit – that all member states comply with our standards and that the Organisation is able to reach out to the remaining potential members (Armenia, Azerbaijan, Belarus, Bosnia and Herzegovina and the Federal Republic of Yugoslavia) to assist them in their legal, political and operational transformation.

To achieve these goals, the Council of Europe has established extensive programmes of co-operation and assistance, initially for the benefit of all new and potential member states. The overriding aim of these programmes is to safeguard and promote democratic reform and stability. Several of our 170 international conventions have paved the way for many European countries aspiring to membership of the European Union.

While the abolition of capital punishment has been envisaged for the last two centuries, the accelerating progress of the abolitionist movement traces its origins to the Universal Declaration of Human Rights of 10 December 1948.

The Council of Europe has been a pioneer in laying down the first binding legal instrument to outlaw capital punishment in peacetime. The Parliamentary Assembly and the Committee of Ministers have subsequently been able to exert political and other pressure to ensure that moratoria on executions have been put in place in countries which still keep the death sentence on their statute books. They have insisted that the states move towards abolition and ratification of Protocol No. 6 to the European Convention on Human Rights.

But the logical continuation of the tendency to restrict the application of the death penalty is total abolition. More recent political developments have facilitated our efforts in that direction.

At the end of the 1990s, it can truly be said that international human rights law has significantly moved forward as far as abolition of the death penalty is concerned.

At the second summit of the Council of Europe (October 1997), the heads of states and governments re-affirmed their attachment to the fundamental principles of the Organisation: pluralist democracy, respect for human rights and the rule of law. They also called for the universal abolition of capital punishment and of the maintenance, in the meantime, of existing moratoria on executions in Europe.

The 102nd Session of the Committee of Ministers (May 1998) "stressed the conviction that priority should be given to obtaining and maintaining a moratorium on executions, to be consolidated as soon as possible by complete abolition of the death penalty". The Committee of Ministers also recognised the necessity of public awareness initiatives on the subject.

The international community has endowed itself with such legal instruments as the Second Optional Protocol to the International Covenant on Civil and Political Rights and Protocol No. 6 to the Convention for the Protection of Human Rights and Fundamental Freedoms, which outlaw capital punishment. But there has also been a progressive recognition that the use of capital punishment has no place in the overall human rights' scheme.

The abolition of capital punishment is at the top of the political agenda of organisations such as the Council of Europe to an extent which can be considered to be one of the major achievements of the international community since the 1993 United Nations World Conference on Human Rights in Vienna.

Today, it is clear that a country seeking membership of the Council of Europe must subscribe to a firm commitment to put into effect an immediate moratorium on executions, to abolish capital punishment within a fixed time-scale, and to sign and ratify Protocol No. 6 – also within a specific time. The latter is required so as to provide an international guarantee against the re-introduction of capital punishment at the whim of whichever political tendency happens to prevail at a given point in time.

These conditions are now part of the core commitments which membership of our Organisation implies. They are relevant not only for the remaining candidate states but also for old and new member states. The recent ratifications of Protocol No. 6 by Greece and Estonia bear witness to this, as does the signature of this instrument by Latvia in June 1998. Moreover, a number of long-standing member states which have abolished capital punishment are now moving towards ratification of Protocol No. 6 (for example Belgium). Other states, which no longer apply the death penalty in practice are heading for full abolition and ratification of Protocol No. 6 (for example the United Kingdom which signed in January 1999). Two of the candidate countries, Armenia and Azerbaijan, have already abolished capital punishment. The other countries which keep the death penalty on their statute books in one form or another – irrespective of whether or not death sentences continue to be handed down – will be expected to follow suit.

The Council of Europe's legal and political mechanisms have been put into effect to ensure that there is only one way ahead on this issue: forward. The process towards abolition within the Council of Europe is irreversible. The recent debate in the Council of Europe's Parliamentary Assembly concerning Russia's and Ukraine's alleged failure to respect their commitment regarding the moratorium on executions is but one example.

The year 1998 was an execution-free zone as far as the Council of Europe member states are concerned.

The Parliamentary Assembly of the Council of Europe has played a key role in securing the abolition of capital punishment. It is therefore most appropriate that a special chapter in this publication is devoted to the work of the Assembly which was at the origin of Protocol No. 6 in 1983. It has adopted successive proposals to outlaw the death penalty, including proposals for a new protocol to ban the death penalty also in time of war. More important-ly, the Assembly has constantly brought pressure to bear on states in order to encourage abolition and – where necessary – insist on moratoria in indi-vidual countries.

It has done so not only in the framework of its examination of applicant countries but also by monitoring compliance of member states with com-mitments on joining the Organisation.

A view prevailing in the Assembly is that states with observer status with the Council of Europe should also adhere to the same principles, values and commitments as those which are required of member states. It is for this rea-son that the Assembly has turned its attention to the situation in Japan and the United States.

The above demonstrates a convergence between the parliamentary and executive branches of the Council of Europe, which together have estab-lished a web of monitoring mechanisms to ensure that the abolitionist process is irreversible.

Generally speaking, abolition of the death penalty is a natural and necessary step on the way towards full integration of European co-operation struc-tures. It is not only the Council of Europe which requires prospective mem-bers to undertake the abolition of the death penalty. For its part, the European Union has made abolition a political pre-condition for member-ship. The Council of Europe and the European Union have agreed to work together to secure abolition.

The European approach to abolition is increasingly being echoed also at the global level. In March 1998, the United Nations Commission on Human Rights adopted a resolution, requesting states which still maintain the death penalty "to establish a moratorium on executions, with a view to complete-ly abolishing the death penalty". This resolution was co-sponsored by many member states of the Council of Europe, including Lithuania, Russia and Ukraine and this text received positive votes of all Council of Europe mem-ber states represented on the United Nations Commission.

It is also significant that the statutes of the International Criminal Tribunals for the former Yugoslavia and for Rwanda, as well as those of the new International Criminal Court, do not provide for capital punishment among their range of sanctions. This is all the more remarkable considering the nature of the crimes which these tribunals are called upon to adjudicate.

For the Council of Europe, capital punishment is incompatible with accepted standards of human rights and dignity and has no place in a democratic society. Our objections are based on the fact that it is an arbitrary, discriminatory and irreversible sanction, and that the brutalisation of society which results from state institutions killing their citizens in the name of justice is a clear consequence of capital punishment.

The European and international communities have consolidated the position of abolition as one of the key human rights issues of the contemporary world and the abolitionist movement is expanding. But we continue to hear the old argument about public opinion against abolition.

The Council of Europe recognises that abolition of the death penalty may not be popular at a time when there is a perception in public opinion that crimes are committed on a scale and in forms unknown in recent history. All too often, the political élites in retentionist countries use such public opinion as an excuse for their own inaction concerning legal and penal reform. It cannot be denied that organised crime plays a very detrimental role, particularly in countries in transition, where the public at large suffers greatly both from direct and very violent crime and – indirectly – from the negative effects of widespread corruption which undermines confidence in democratic institutions. In these circumstances, popular opinion easily falls prey to populist messages of "getting tough" on criminals rather than accepting more sophisticated arguments such as the need to give proper thought to effective legal and social policies for the reduction of serious crime.

Many pro-death penalty opinions among the public are based on inaccurate information and/or false assumptions. This is why continuous attempts are being made to ensure public awareness of the negative aspects of the death penalty. This is also why the Council of Europe is offering assistance and support for governmental as well as non-governmental initiatives aimed at provoking public debate which allows the facts to be dissected rather than to advance simplistic emotional assumptions. In this way we seek to address common misconceptions about the death penalty. For example, the death penalty is still frequently seen as an effective measure to curb serious crime. The public should be made aware of the fact that all data and research on the subject show that abolition has no negative impact on crime rates. On the contrary, there is evidence to show that the reintroduction, or stepping up, of the death penalty has done nothing to curb serious crime. The so-called "deterrent" effect of the death penalty is a fallacy and should be presented as such.

It is often said that the death penalty is an important tool in the context of combating international organised crime. In fact the mere existence of the death penalty can constitute an obstacle to international co-operation. For example, before abolition, France encountered serious problems when requesting the extradition of criminals from countries which had abolished the death penalty because the latter wanted guarantees that their prisoners would not be executed.

Another equally flawed pro-death penalty argument is its cost-effectiveness. It is claimed that recourse to the death penalty is less onerous than keeping criminals in jail. If the real issue is money one must consider the global prison situation. For example, the Russian Federation currently has approximately 1 000 persons on death row while the total population of persons in prison or other forms of incarceration is close to 1 million. Reference has also been made to the chronic problem of overcrowding in prisons and it is said that abolition of the death penalty would require the construction of new prisons.

However, if economics were the real issue, it would be more appropriate to look at the rate and duration of confinement of the vast number of persons detained for far less serious offences or who are awaiting trial. The introduction of a diversified sentencing policy – including alternatives to detention – as well as limited recourse to detention on remand, would certainly lead to much greater financial savings.

The death penalty is irreversible and the risk of judicial error can never be entirely ruled out. The representatives of the judiciary are particularly well placed to understand this risk. This is perhaps one reason why, increasingly, the judiciary has put a final stop to executions. In 1989, the Hungarian Constitutional Court ruled that the death penalty clashed with the human rights provisions of the constitution. In 1995, the Constitutional Court of South Africa, in one of its first judgments, declared the death penalty unconstitutional, thereby instantly saving the lives of 453 inmates on death row. Let us hope that these acts against the death penalty will be followed in other countries. The Human Rights Chamber for Bosnia and Herzegovina last year effectively barred an execution, ruling that the carrying out of a death sentence by a military court in Sarajevo in 1993 would violate Protocol No. 6 of the European Convention on Human Rights and thereby also breach Bosnia's obligations under the Dayton Peace Agreement.[1]

The courts in retentionist countries can play a potentially important role. They can set the tone by exercising self-restraint and by refraining from handing down capital sentences on the basis of existing Criminal Code provisions.

---

1. Decision of the Human Rights Chamber (case of *Damjanović v. The Federation of Bosnia and Herzegovina*) of 5 September 1997, case No. CH/96/30.

In our efforts to move towards full European abolition and taking Protocol No. 6 of the European Convention on Human Rights as the basis, it is extremely important to focus the debate on facts and on providing objective information. Indeed, there is a tendency among die-hard retentionists to dismiss arguments supporting abolition as emotional and even irrational. Rather than give in to cries for revenge – a death for a death – we must take one step back and work to make sure that, as the guilty are punished for their crimes, their punishment reflects the choices of a civilised, democratic society.

Our task is to make sure that abolition is part of a series of measures to develop a more humane penal system which will enable serious crime to be effectively tackled: to provide credible alternatives to the death penalty in a post-abolition context; to reduce the prison population and improve the material conditions of detention; to provide adequate assistance to victims of serious crime and to allow the rehabilitation of both victims and offenders.

The Council of Europe considers that there is no rationale behind, nor any justification for, the death penalty. It simply has no place in a society with a civilised penal system. No one has encapsulated this better in recent times than the Director of Human Rights of the Council of Europe, Mr Pierre Henri Imbert, when he said:

> "Revenge is kindred with our nature and our instincts but not with the law. The law cannot obey the same rules as human nature. Murder may come naturally to mankind, but the law is not made to imitate or reproduce nature. The law is crafted to correct nature."

Protocol No. 6 of the European Convention on Human Rights, the jurisprudence based on that protocol, and any future instrument which the Council of Europe can adopt to establish a total ban on capital punishment, are all part of that law.

6. THE DEATH PENALTY AND THE CASE-LAW OF THE INSTITUTIONS OF THE EUROPEAN CONVENTION ON HUMAN RIGHTS

Caroline Ravaud, Senior lawyer, Registry of the European Court of Human Rights and Stefan Trechsel, President, European Commission of Human Rights

This chapter presents a view of the case-law of the mechanisms of the Convention, particularly concerning the right to life, the prevention of torture and inhuman or degrading treatment and the abolition of the death penalty, specified in Protocol No. 6 of the Convention.

The first paragraph of Article 2 of the Convention for the Protection of Human Rights and Fundamental Freedoms, which was signed in Rome on 4 November 1950 and came into force on 3 September 1953 after having been ratified by ten states, provides:

> "Everyone's right to life shall be protected by law. No one shall be deprived of his life intentionally save in the execution of a sentence of a court following his conviction of a crime for which this penalty is provided by law."

The second paragraph of Article 2 gives a restrictive list of cases where deprivation of life is not considered to have been inflicted in breach of that article because it results from the use of force rendered absolutely necessary either in order to defend a person from unlawful violence, or to effect a lawful arrest or prevent the escape of a person lawfully detained, or to lawfully take action for the purpose of quelling a riot or insurrection.

The primary object of this second paragraph is not to define instances where it would be permissible intentionally to kill someone, in contrast with the first paragraph; it merely describes situations where it is permitted to use force, which may result, as an unintended outcome, in the loss of life. The use of force must be absolutely necessary for the achievement of one of the three purposes set out in paragraph 2 of Article 2, and therefore, when examining the cases brought before it, the European Court of Human Rights has assessed the acts under consideration not only in themselves but also in the light of their planning and control.

The precedents established by the European Court of Human Rights as regards Article 2 of the Convention have mainly concerned cases involving possible exceptions to the right to life.[1] There is no judgment that deals with imposition of the death penalty.

The right to life and the ban on torture or inhuman or degrading treatment or punishment, contained in Article 3 of the Convention, are among the most fundamental rights which states must secure to everyone within their jurisdiction. It should here be noted that the Convention does not seek to protect individuals against other individuals' acts infringing their fundamental rights; no convention can prevent murder, incest, rape, armed robbery or any other act of violence perpetrated by one individual against another.

The Convention merely aims to define and control the action or measures which public authorities are permitted to take in breach of individuals' fundamental rights, for the good of society as a whole. From this standpoint, the Convention, like many international legal instruments, is a pledge of good conduct given by states which, at least in theory, have a monopoly on the lawful use of violence. The main difference from other international commitments to safeguard human rights entered into by the majority of states lies in the fact that the states of Europe have, subject to certain conditions, agreed to be bound by a mechanism for the judicial review of action or measures taken in breach of their obligations.

Although, in the event of war or other public emergency threatening the life of the nation, Article 15 allows states to take measures derogating from their obligations under the Convention, to the extent strictly required by the exigencies of the situation, no derogation with regard to the right to life is permitted, except in respect of deaths resulting from lawful acts of war. Nor is it possible to exclude the operation of the ban on torture, servitude or slavery, set forth in Article 4, or the provisions of Article 7 prohibiting punishment without law (*nulla poena sine lege* – the principle that a person can only be found guilty of an offence recognised by law and that the penalty imposed must be prescribed by law). The ban on taking

---

1. See, for example, the *McCann and Others v. the United Kingdom* judgment of 27 September 1995, which concerned the killing by the United Kingdom special forces of three alleged IRA terrorists, suspected of preparing to carry out a car bomb attack in Gibraltar. The Court held (by ten votes to nine) that there had been a violation of Article 2 on account of the authorities' negligence with regard to the organisation and control of the operation. For an opposite line of reasoning, see the *Andronicou and Constantinou v. Cyprus* judgment of 9 October 1997, concerning action by special forces to release a young woman being held hostage by her partner, which led to the shooting of both young people.

measures derogating from Article 2 may, however, be undermined in respect of the death penalty, in that the requirement of a fair trial stipulated in Article 6 is not included on the list of hard-core guarantees. Would it be acceptable in time of war for a court which was neither independent nor impartial, and which in no way respected the defendant's right to a fair hearing, to sentence someone to death? In our opinion, the answer must be no. If such derogations were allowed it would virtually be to no avail to protect the right to life, and this is what Article 15, paragraph 2, in fact seeks to avoid.

As we have seen, capital punishment, which is expressly provided for in Article 2 of the 1950 Convention, is the only instance where intentional deprivation of life is permissible. Although a death sentence may be pronounced only in the cases provided by law, following a fair trial before an independent, impartial tribunal, as required under Article 6, it is still a homicide committed in cold blood for the greater public good. The fact that the death penalty might be considered morally right on the ground that crime must be punished or that society must be protected from those who break its rules[1] does not make the slightest difference; nor does the never-ending debate on the value of capital punishment as a means of dissuasion. To the best of our knowledge, no scientific study has so far provided the slightest element of proof that capital punishment in any way acts as a deterrent.

The so-called "civilised" countries have long done away with the torments, such as the wheel, quartering or the stake, which used to be inflicted on offenders before they were put to death. Extracting confessions through torture is no longer used as a means of obtaining evidence of guilt, at least in law if not necessarily in fact, and there are no more public executions. Similarly, developments in criminal law have increasingly limited the list of crimes punishable by the death penalty, and countries where it is still applicable reserve it for the most barbaric offences against the person. It was inevitable that this change in standards would raise the question of whether the death penalty itself should not simply be abolished.

---

1. Article 2267 of the final version of the new catechism of the Catholic Church, an 848 page document published in French on 13 October 1998 (see the issue of *Le Monde* of the same date), reads:
"The Church's traditional teaching does not preclude capital punishment, where the offender's identity and liability have been fully ascertained and it is the only viable means of effectively safeguarding human life from undue assault. However, if non-violent means suffice to defend and protect individuals against assault the authority should settle for such means ... Nowadays, given the state's means of effectively punishing crime and rendering offenders incapable of doing further harm, without permanently depriving them of the possibility of repenting, instances where it is absolutely necessary to end an offender's life are rare, if not all but non-existent."

At European level the will to abolish the death penalty led to the drafting of Protocol No. 6 to the Convention, which was opened for signature in April 1983 and came into force on 1 March 1985 after having been ratified by five states. This Protocol No. 6 was largely a result of the stubborn determination shown by Mr Christian Broda when he held office as Austria's Minister for Justice. In the preamble to the protocol, the signatory states note that "the evolution that has occurred in several member states of the Council of Europe expresses a general tendency in favour of abolition of the death penalty."

The first states to ratify the protocol were Denmark, Austria, Sweden, Spain and Luxembourg.

France abolished the death penalty in October 1981 but did not ratify Protocol No. 6 until February 1986. A number of other countries, which had long done away with the death penalty in their domestic law, were also slow to ratify the protocol: Switzerland, where use of the death penalty in time of peace had been abandoned as far back as 1942, ratified it only in October 1987; Portugal, where abolition had taken place in 1976, did so in October 1986. Belgium, which had signed the protocol as far back as 1983, ratified it only on 10 December 1998, although no civilian had been executed there since 1863, as a death sentence was automatically commuted to extended imprisonment through a royal pardon. Moreover, the death penalty had been abolished by an Act of 10 July 1996.

Today, among the founder members of the Council of Europe – which now has forty-one member states – Turkey alone has neither signed nor ratified the protocol, although it is *de facto* an abolitionist state. This can be seen not only from the fact that no one has been hanged in Turkey since 1984, but also from parliament's failure to confirm the enforcement of the approximately 300 death sentences passed since 1984, with the result that, through operation of the early release system, an offender sentenced to death will at most serve eighteen years in prison. The Republic of Cyprus, which joined the Council of Europe in May 1961, has also not ratified Protocol No. 6 – though it has signed it – whereas it has already abolished capital punishment in time of peace.

Greece ratified the protocol very recently, in September 1998, and the United Kingdom has only just signed it (January 1999). Such delay is difficult to comprehend, given that the United Kingdom has not hanged anyone since the 1960s and, under an Act of 1965, the death penalty still exists only for a limited number of crimes such as treason, piracy and committing adultery with the wife of the monarch's eldest son.

Among the states which have become members of the Organisation since 1989 and have ratified the European Convention on Human Rights – mainly central and eastern European countries – only Albania, Lithuania, Bulgaria, Poland, Russia, Latvia and Ukraine have yet to ratify the protocol. Of the latter states, only Russia and Ukraine still have capital punishment, although they seem to be applying a *de facto* moratorium, whereas Poland has already abolished the death penalty, and in Albania, Bulgaria, Lithuania and Latvia the moratorium is official. These have been official decisions of the parliaments of the respective countries.[1]

The general tendency towards abolition of the death penalty in Europe – whether *de facto* or *de jure* – has led the Parliamentary Assembly of the Council of Europe to require states wishing to join the Organisation to give a firm, solemn undertaking that they will apply a moratorium on executions until the death penalty is abolished in their states, which should take place within three years of joining the Council of Europe.[2] Ukraine, which became a member of the Organisation on 9 November 1995, is currently threatened with sanctions by the Assembly for having failed to observe the moratorium. Although executions were covered by official secrets legislation, and there are therefore no reliable statistics or official information on the number performed, it would seem that a total of about 180 executions took place in Ukraine in 1996 and 1997.

The Assembly's firm stance, albeit praiseworthy, can be justified only on the ground that it serves as a reminder to the states concerned of the importance of honouring their commitments: both Russia and Ukraine gave their word that they would apply a moratorium and abolish capital punishment as soon as possible. The question whether, given the state of development of these countries which are making the transition to democracy and encountering huge economic and social problems, it was not premature and unrealistic to require them to abide by a rule which many other European countries had taken decades to adopt in domestic and in European law, was apparently not raised, doubtless so as not to fuel criticism that these countries were being granted favourable treatment.

According to information released by the Ministry of Justice in October 1998, Russia, which has been a member of the Organisation since 28 February 1996,

---

1. See the report of the Committee on Legal Affairs and Human Rights of the Parliamentary Assembly entitled "Europe: a death penalty-free continent", Appendix III.

2. The Parliamentary Assembly allowed Ukraine a three-year time-limit for ratifying Protocol No. 6: see paragraph 12.ii of its Opinion No. 190 (1995) on Ukraine's application for membership. On the other hand, in its Opinion No. 209 (1999) on Georgia's application for membership, submitted on 14 July 1996, the Assembly fixed a time-limit of only one year, but Georgia had already abolished capital punishment in the autumn of 1997 after instituting a moratorium in February 1995.

has about 839 prisoners who have been sentenced to death. Executions have reportedly ceased since August 1996 (apart from one in Chechnya in 1998), but no official moratorium has been instituted. However, according to a statement by Amnesty International, in a ruling of 2 February 1999 the Constitutional Court of the Russian Federation banned the courts from issuing death sentences in cases not heard by a jury. The trial-by-jury system has currently been introduced in only nine of the Federation's eighty-nine regions. Amnesty therefore regards this decision as amounting to a *de facto* abolition of the death penalty.

Protocol No. 6 is also a source of law for countries not members of the Council of Europe, and therefore not parties to the Convention. Annex 6 of the Dayton Peace Agreement of 1995, which ended the war in Bosnia-Herzegovina, set up a Commission on Human Rights, consisting of an ombudsman and a Human Rights Chamber for Bosnia and Herzegovina, the newly-formed state consisting of two entities, the Federation of Bosnia and Herzegovina and the Republika Srpska. Both the ombudsman and the Human Rights Chamber have jurisdiction to consider "alleged or apparent violations of human rights as provided in the Convention for the Protection of Human Rights and Fundamental Freedoms and the protocols thereto ...".[1]

For example, in April 1997 the Human Rights Chamber, which sits in Sarajevo, found admissible an application alleging violations of Protocol No. 6 and of Article 3 of the Convention, which had been lodged against the Federation of Bosnia and Herzegovina by a person sentenced to death by a military court in 1993 for the murder of three people.[2]

With what is, after all, a fairly widespread abolitionist tendency in modern-day Europe, what contribution can the Convention institutions make? Is there still scope for them to take a position on capital punishment?

Protocol No. 6 is worded in absolute terms, since Article 1 quite bluntly states "the death penalty shall be abolished" and continues "no one shall be condemned to such penalty or executed".

Article 2 then goes on to provide that this absolute ban on capital punishment shall not prevent states from making provision in their law for the death penalty to apply in respect of acts committed in time of war or of imminent threat of war.

It quite logically follows that a state which has, necessarily, already abolished the death penalty in its domestic law merely makes that abolition official by

---

1. See Article II, paragraph 2, of Annex 6 to the Dayton Agreement.
2. See Application No. CH/96/30, *Damjanović v. Federation of Bosnia and Herzegovina*, decision of 11 April 1997.

ratifying the protocol to the Convention. It also follows that, at least in respect of all acts previously punishable by death in time of peace, the Strasbourg institutions should no longer be asked to deal with applications alleging a violation of the protocol. As soon as it ratifies that instrument, a state commits itself not only to halt all executions, but also no longer to sentence anyone to death. Indeed, in those circumstances handing down a death sentence would inevitably also constitute a breach of Article 7 of the Convention.

The case-law of the Strasbourg institutions (that is to say the European Commission of Human Rights and the former European Court of Human Rights, which were operational until 1 November 1998, when they were replaced by a new single, permanent Court) has mainly come into being through active interpretation of the guarantees afforded by Article 3 of the Convention.

Well before Protocol No. 6 was drafted and came into force, the question arose whether the death penalty, provided for in Article 2 of the Convention, might be regarded as "inhuman or degrading treatment or punishment" within the meaning of Article 3. No application ever questioned the methods of execution used in countries where capital punishment still existed (such as the garrotte in Spain or the guillotine in France), but very early on the Commission had to deal with applications alleging a breach of Article 3 in the event of the applicants' expulsion or extradition to a third country where they were liable to be executed on arrival, or to be subjected to torture or to inhuman or degrading treatment.

It took the view that, in exceptional circumstances, a problem might be posed under Article 3 of the Convention if the intention was to extradite a person to a country where "due to the very nature of the regime of that country or to a particular situation in that country, basic human rights ... might be either grossly violated or entirely suppressed."[1] This approach was based on the reasoning that under Article 1 the states undertook to secure the rights and freedoms guaranteed by the Convention to "everyone within their jurisdiction", which was the case of persons whom a state planned to extradite, deport or turn back, with the result that the protection afforded by Article 3 of the Convention extended to the obligation not to place such a person in an irremediable situation of objective danger even outside a state's jurisdiction.[2]

---

1. See Application No. 1802/62, *X v. the Federal Republic of Germany*, Yearbook 6, pp. 462 to 480.
2. For a case of extradition to Turkey, which at the time had not yet recognised the right of individual petition provided for in the former Article 25 of the Convention, see Application No. 10308/83, *Altun v. the Federal Republic of Germany*, decision of 3 May 1983, DR (Decisions and Reports) 36, p. 209.

One of the most sensitive cases examined by the Commission was that of *Amekrane v. the United Kingdom* (Application No. 5961/72). This application was lodged by the widow and children of a Moroccan officer who, after a failed attempt at a *coup d'état* in his country, had sought refuge in Gibraltar and whom the United Kingdom authorities had handed over to the Moroccan authorities the very next day. The officer was subsequently tried by a Moroccan court martial for his role in the attempted seizure of power, found guilty and shot. In 1974 an amicable settlement was reached, whereby the United Kingdom Government agreed to pay the widow and children a sum of 35 000 pounds sterling as compensation.

This instance of extra-territorial application of the Convention was all the more unusual in that the Convention does not guarantee foreigners any right, as such, not to be extradited or expelled, and such an approach amounts to holding a state bound by the Convention liable for the fate inflicted on an individual by a state not party thereto. The state which expels or extradites the individual will be exculpated only if it can show that it obtained full assurances from the country of destination that no treatment contrary to Article 3 would actually be meted out.

Most of the cases examined by the Court have concerned allegations of a risk of torture or inhuman or degrading treatment in the country to which an individual was to be removed.[1]

The best known case brought before the European Court of Human Rights in the field of extradition is that of *Soering v. the United Kingdom*.[2] Jens Soering, a German national who at the material time was 18 years old, was arrested in the United Kingdom in April 1986, along with his girlfriend, in connection with a routine case of cheque fraud. In August of the same year the United States requested the couple's extradition under the terms of the extradition treaty of 1972 between the two countries. The applicant was to face trial in the State of Virginia on charges of having murdered his girl-friend's parents (who were against their relationship) by repeated stabbing, a crime committed in March 1985, allegedly while the couple were prey to a *folie à deux*.

If he had been found guilty of capital murder, after having been extradited, he would have been liable to be sentenced to death by electrocution, the

---

1. See, for example, the Court's judgments in the cases of *Cruz Varas* (expulsion to Chile, no violation) and *Paez* (expulsion to Peru, case struck off the list after the measure had been cancelled), both brought against Sweden, and in the case of *Chahal v. the United Kingdom* (expulsion of a Sikh to India, violation).
2. Judgment of 7 July 1989, Series A No. 161.

punishment for that class of offence in Virginia, which had resumed executions in 1977 following a moratorium of several years.

In view of the wording of Article 2 of the Convention, it was not possible to contend that the death penalty *per se* breached Article 3. The Court therefore confirmed that the extradition of a person to a state where that person risked the death penalty did not in itself raise an issue under either Article 2 or Article 3, despite evolving standards in western Europe regarding the existence and use of capital punishment.

The Court pointed out that, although *de facto* the death penalty no longer existed in the contracting states, they had chosen to amend the Convention by preparing a specific protocol on abolition, and it was therefore not possible to interpret Article 3 as generally prohibiting the death penalty as inhuman or degrading treatment or punishment.

However, in the case under consideration, the applicant did not complain of a breach of Article 3 by reason of the almost certain imposition of the death penalty, but did so on the ground that, in his contention, his exposure to the "death-row phenomenon" would result in inhuman and degrading treatment. Under American law, it is possible to lodge a number of appeals against enforcement of a death sentence, which may therefore be deferred several times. In paragraph 56 of its judgment, the Court noted that the average time between trial and execution in Virginia, calculated on the basis of the seven executions which had taken place since 1977, was six to eight years, and that the delays were primarily due to a strategy by convicted prisoners to prolong the appeal proceedings as much as possible.

The Court recalled that ill-treatment, including punishment, must attain a minimum level of severity to fall within the scope of Article 3, and that the assessment of this minimum was, in the nature of things, relative since it depended on all the circumstances of the case, such as the nature and context of the treatment or punishment, the manner and method of its execution, its duration, its physical or mental effects and, in some instances, the sex, age and state of health of the victim.

In Mr Soering's case the Court held that, despite the procedural guarantees offered to him in the United States, having regard to the very long period of time spent on death row, with the ever present and mounting anguish of awaiting execution of the death penalty, and to the personal circumstances of the applicant, especially his age and mental state at the time of the offence, his extradition to the United States would expose him to a real risk of treatment going beyond the threshold set by Article 3.

It should be noted that, since the United Kingdom had not ratified Protocol No. 6, the question whether extradition or deportation to a country applying the death penalty would, as with Article 3, render the extraditing or deporting state liable for having breached the protocol did not arise in the *Soering* proceedings. On the other hand, the Commission considered this issue in another case concerning extradition to the United States, brought against France, which had ratified the protocol.[1] After examining the firm assurances obtained by the French Government not only from the federal authorities, but also, and above all, from the prosecuting authorities of the State of Texas, who had promised not to seek the death penalty in the murder proceedings brought against the applicant, the Commission was of the opinion that those assurances were such as to eliminate the danger of the applicant's being sentenced to death and that extradition should therefore not expose her to a serious risk of treatment or punishment contrary to Article 3 or to Article 1 of Protocol No. 6.

From this point of view, the *Aylor-Davis* case differed considerably from the *Soering* case, where the United Kingdom Government had only been able to obtain from the Commonwealth's Attorney (the Virginia prosecuting authority) an undertaking to make a representation to the judge at the time of sentencing that it was the wish of the United Kingdom that the death penalty should not be imposed or carried out, an undertaking which the Court deemed insufficient to eliminate all risk of execution of the death penalty.

In the current state of the case-law it therefore cannot be inferred that any measure extraditing someone to the United States would pose a problem under the Convention, whether owing to the existence of the "death-row phenomenon" or because that country retains the death penalty. A cynic might even interpret the *Soering* judgment as meaning that provided a person condemned to death is executed promptly no problem is posed in respect of the Convention.

In some of the most recent cases, which have not yet been judged by the new European Court of Human Rights, the Court will probably be obliged to go beyond the principles laid down in the *Soering* judgment. For instance, two applications have been brought against Bulgaria,[2] concerning persons sentenced to death in 1989. Bulgaria has been applying a moratorium since 1990, but no law abolishing the death penalty has yet been passed, and many members of parliament wish to reinstate executions. When the question of resuming executions is regularly raised in parliament, the applicants complain of violations of Articles 2 and 3 of the Convention, arguing, *inter*

---

1. Application No. 22742/93, *Joy Aylor-Davis v. France*, decision of 20 January 1994, DR 76-A, p. 164.
2. Applications Nos. 40653/98, *Iorgov v. Bulgaria*, and 42346/98, *Belchinov v. Bulgaria*.

alia, that they were sentenced to death as the outcome of proceedings which did not satisfy the minimum guarantees of a fair trial, that, if they were to be executed, this would in itself amount to a violation of Article 3 and, above all, that Article 3 is breached as a result of the prolonged uncertainty about their fate, which has lasted almost nine years. Their situation is exacerbated by the poor conditions in which they are being detained.

The issue of the poor conditions under which persons sentenced to death are imprisoned is also raised in a number of applications brought against Ukraine,[1] and the Commission has already had occasion to visit Ukraine in order to inspect the prison where they are being held.

Established precedents in many Council of Europe member states in fact go much further than the case-law of the European Court of Human Rights. At least in matters of extradition, where the bilateral treaties permit the requested state to pose a number of conditions, certain national courts have established the principle that extradition must be refused not only in cases where there is a risk that the death penalty will be carried out, but also where the law of the state requesting extradition merely provides that a capital sentence may be imposed. As far back as 1979 the Italian Constitutional Court refused to allow a person's extradition to France on the ground that the charges brought against the offender in France then carried the death penalty, which Italy had abolished under Article 27, paragraph 4, of the Constitution of 1948. Similarly, in 1987 the French *Conseil d'Etat* cancelled extradition orders against persons liable to be sentenced to death in Turkey and Algeria, on the ground that handing them over to those countries would be contrary to French public policy.[2]

Many other examples could be cited. It is clear that there is now a sort of moral consensus among the member states that any extradition request must be subjected to extremely close scrutiny to determine whether the available guarantees that the death sentence will not be enforced are sufficient. Even then, the best guarantee is that the state requesting extradition should not issue any death sentence at all. For instance, the United Kingdom Government, which was obliged to comply with the *Soering* judgment and could not retain the applicant on its territory indefinitely, decided to make

---

1. See, for instance, Application No. 38812/97, *Poltoratskiy v. Ukraine.*
2. See the *Fidan* judgment of 27 February 1987, *recueil Lebon*, p. 81, and the *Gacem* judgment of 14 December 1987, op. cit., p. 733. It should, however, be noted that in these two judgments, as in the *Bamohammed* judgment of 1985, the *Conseil d'Etat* still made reference to the lack of sufficient assurances from the requesting states' authorities that the executions would not be carried out.
3. See Resolution DH (90) 8, dated 12 March 1990, of the Committee of Ministers of the Council of Europe, which, under the Convention, is the organ responsible for supervising execution of the Court's judgments; it can be noted in passing that Mr Soering was finally sentenced to ninety-nine years' imprisonment.

Mr Soering's extradition to the United States conditional on an undertaking that he would be charged not with capital murder, but only with first degree murder, an offence which did not carry the death sentence. This condition was accepted by the United States authorities.[3]

7. THE UNITED NATIONS AND THE ABOLITION OF THE DEATH PENALTY

Roberto Toscano, Co-ordinator of Policy Planning Activities, Ministry of Foreign Affairs, Rome

> *"Why this disgusting, pointless, unnecessary insult?"*
> (Fyodor Dostoevsky, *The Idiot*)

Few issues are as politically delicate and ethically charged as the question of capital punishment. This is so not only because of the evident primacy of matters of life and death in moral and political discourse, but because capital punishment is not simply about death, but about death decreed and administered by the state on behalf of the entire community, and justified on the basis of the imperatives of protection of members of the community against unjust harm.

But this immediately reveals the most fundamental, most glaring contradiction – a contradiction the awareness of which, ever more widespread in contemporary society, is perhaps the main argument undermining the foundations of this ancient practice.

In fact, it would be difficult to challenge Hobbes when he wrote in 1651 that men accept the restraints that life in a society ("commonwealth") implies, because of "the foresight of their own preservation".[1] In other words, human society can be seen as a "covenant against death", a common, co-operative endeavour to resist, to postpone, the inevitable outcome of human existence. For that purpose social man has developed not only institutional mechanisms (of which the modern nation-state is but the latest instance), but also moral norms, the most fundamental of which is "Thou Shalt Not Kill". The death penalty contradicts both the basic "anti-death" function of human society and the concomitant moral principles.[2]

---

1. Thomas Hobbes, (1996) *Leviathan*. Oxford/New York: Oxford University Press, p. 111.
2. "It is written: 'Thou shalt not kill', and now, since someone killed, should he be killed as well? No, that's not right." (Fyodor Dostoevsky, *The Idiot*, Vol. I, chapter 2). In the same novel, Dostoevsky paints in stark, definitive colours the unsurpassed horror – as we know, on the basis of his unique personal experience of a last-moment reprieve – entailed by that certainty of death that is the cruel lot of those who are to be executed. It seems difficult, after reading his testimony, to define the death penalty as other than "cruel and unusual punishment."

Of course, the contradiction is not specific to capital punishment, but characterises the entire range of moral and political dilemmas arising from the problem of violence. Peace is an avowed universal goal (except for aberrant theories such as nazi ideology), and yet the goal of peace has been (and is being) used to justify sustained levels of armaments and even acts of aggression. And of course one can always find a handy item of Roman wisdom to support this: *Si vis pacem, para bellum* (If you want peace, prepare for war).

Those who uphold the need for capital punishment are motivated basically from the same ideological grounds, though they certainly would not be brave enough to formulate it as clearly, that is to say: *Si vis vitam, para mortem* (If you want life, prepare for death). Yet, the logic is exactly the same. A faulty and disingenuous logic, actually, since peace and life can be defended, must be defended, with strength that is short of war and short of death. Since one must reject the false alternative between a ferocious society on one side and a defenceless one on the other.

The parallel is a of course an asymmetrical one, since the goal of achieving international security without war is made problematic (though by no means impossible) by the absence of centralised enforcement mechanisms; those mechanisms that constitute, on the other hand, the very essence of the modern nation-state – a state which must be able to ensure to its citizens protection of life without denial of life.

Why the United Nations?

If the issue of the death penalty, of its abolition or retention, is so charged with political and moral implications, then why should we not be content with addressing it within each individual society, or at the most among groupings of nations that are more homogeneous in culture and traditions, or even – as in the case of Europe – actually converging in terms of institution-building and common ethos? Does it make any sense to try a global, worldwide approach to such a controversial issue? And, in concrete terms, why should there be a United Nations role of any sort in addressing this issue?

The apparent common sense of this objection hides a very dangerous unspoken assumption: that of the impossibility of a common human endeavour in addressing common human problems. An assumption whose acceptance would make the very existence of the United Nations useless if not inconceivable.

We will try to reverse this assumption, and state that in so far as the question of capital punishment touches upon the most basic of all human rights, the right to life, saying that the United Nations has no mandate to deal with it would be tantamount to saying that the United Nations has no mandate to deal with human rights. In order to dismiss such a suggestion it is enough to read the very first lines of the preamble of the United Nations Charter. Soon after the determination "to save succeeding generations from the scourge of war" we find, in fact, as the second basic purpose of the United Nations "to reaffirm faith in fundamental human rights, in the dignity and worth of the human person." If it is true that the charter itself did not develop either the identification of those rights or the machinery to promote and protect them, the charter did work as a premise for a subsequent substantial evolution in terms of both principles and norms.

As far as the specific issue of the death penalty is concerned, we will briefly list only the most basic steps in this evolutionary process:

- the Universal Declaration of Human Rights (1948) identified the right to life (together with the right to liberty and security of person) among the most basic human rights;

- the International Covenant on Civil and Political Rights (ICCPR) (1966) states: "Every human being has the inherent right to life," and goes on to add "no one shall be arbitrarily deprived of his life". The ICCPR – a normative, and not a simple declarative text – addresses specifically capital punishment in order to introduce a series of conditions and limitations, that is:
  - it can be imposed only for "the most serious crimes";
  - it must be the result of a "final judgment" (meaning that there should be a provision for appealing a death sentence);
  - it must be imposed by the sentence of a "competent court";
  - it must be the result of the application of a law that was in force at the moment the crime was committed;
  - it must not be imposed on persons younger than 18 years of age;
  - it must not be carried out on pregnant women;
  - the request for pardon or commutation is a right.

The Second Optional Protocol to the ICCPR (1989) goes beyond this regulatory/restrictive approach to embrace an openly abolitionist goal. Its Article 1 reads in fact: "No one within the jurisdiction of a State Party to the present Protocol shall be executed," and continues: "each State Party shall take all necessary measures to abolish the death penalty within its jurisdiction".

Although only thirty-one states have so far ratified the protocol, it can be said that the abolitionist seed has been firmly planted in United Nations' soil, and that the question is not about whether, but only when it will bear its full fruit.

"Gallant folly" in Geneva

The soil is available and fertile (the role and normative activity of the United Nations in the field of human rights), the seed has been planted (the limitations on the application of the death penalty introduced in the ICCPR – and in later conventions; the abolitionist "window of opportunity" opened by the Second Optional Protocol to the ICCPR). And yet it has been clear for several years that there is no automatic progression to the eventual abolitionist victory, and especially that the pace of advancement of the abolitionist cause will be decided not only by cultural trends, but also by determined political action.

Several countries (especially in Europe) share the commitment to the abolitionist cause, but in the United Nations framework it was Italy that took it upon itself (greeted at the beginning by widespread if not universal scepticism, even on the part of the like-minded on the issue) to exert the role of initiator.[1]

The first round of this battle took place at the 49th Session of the United Nations General Assembly, in 1994, when Italy presented a resolution with an abolitionist inspiration (though with a gradualistic approach) that was literally amended to death. A defeat, certainly, and one that was taken by critics and sceptics as evidence of the quixotic nature of Italy's attempt.

And yet the 1994 defeat set the foundations for the 1997 victory; not only because the issue was out of the closet, and some serious political thinking had been set in motion in several capitals, but also because in 1994, in New York, the issue was channelled through the Third Committee (Social, Humanitarian and Cultural) – being thus defined as a human rights issue – and not through the Sixth (Legal), as maintained by the opponents of the Italian initiative, who defined it as a merely legal issue.

The road to Geneva, and to the Commission on Human Rights, was open.

---

1. For a detailed account of Italy's initiatives on capital punishment see: Leonardo Bencini (1997) "Le Nazioni Unite e l'abolizione della pena di morte: recenti iniziative," *La Comunita' Internazionale*, No. 2, p. 299.

On 3 April 1997, the Commission on Human Rights approved Resolution 1997/12, ("Question of the Death Penalty"), presented by Italy with 45 other countries co-sponsoring: votes in favour were 27, with 11 against and 14 abstentions.[1]

The vote took place in an atmosphere of expectation and tension, especially since the opponents of the resolution tried to stop it by presenting seven different amendments that (as the Italian delegation stated in order to maintain the cohesion of the supporters of the initiative) would have, if approved, distorted and nullified the import of the resolution. The result was greeted by true surprise. It is interesting to quote here a comment published in the aftermath of the session in the newsletter of one of the most militant abolitionist NGOs, the Quakers: "No one believed that this resolution would pass. Since a similar resolution had been defeated in the General Assembly only two years before, most considered it a foolhardy mistake or a gallant but forlorn hope ... Who was the gallant fool? Italy."[2]

The text of the resolution combines an unabashedly abolitionist goal with a moderate, gradualist approach. It calls upon all states to abide by the existing international norms regulating and limiting the application of the death penalty; it also "calls upon all states that have not yet abolished the death penalty progressively to restrict the number of offences for which the death penalty may be imposed"; and finally it "calls upon the same states to consider suspending execution, with a view to completely abolishing the death penalty."

The combination of radical ends with moderate means proved to be a winning strategy, since it allowed Italy to enlarge (with the determinant support of its EU partners and other delegations, especially Latin American) the scope of consensus even beyond the abolitionist hard core. This chapter, however, does not intend to narrate a diplomatic history of the many negotiations (both in Geneva and in other capitals), alliances, compromises, confrontations, that lie behind the approval of the 1997 resolution, and of the one that, drafted in basically similar terms, was approved at the 1998 Convention on Human Rights.[3] Rather, it intends to focus on some basic political aspects whose interest goes way beyond the contingent events in Geneva.

---

1. *In favour*: Angola, Argentina, Austria, Belarus, Brazil, Bulgaria, Canada, Cape Verde, Chile, Colombia, Czech Republic, Denmark, Dominican Republic, Ecuador, France, Germany, Ireland, Italy, Mexico, Mozambique, Nepal, Netherlands, Nicaragua, Russian Federation, South Africa, Ukraine, Uruguay.
Against: Algeria, Bangladesh, Bhutan, China, Egypt, Indonesia, Japan, Malaysia, Pakistan, Republic of Korea, United States of America.
Abstaining: Benin, Cuba, El Salvador, Ethiopia, Gabon, Guinea, India, Madagascar, Philippines, Sri Lanka, Uganda, United Kingdom, Zaire, Zimbabwe.
2. Rachel Brett (1997) "Gallant Folly in Geneva," *The Friend*, 9 May, p. 6.
3. Resolution 1998/12 was approved at the 54th Session of the CHR on 30 March 1998.

In order to grasp fully the political essence of the debate on the death penalty, it is important to examine the basic arguments that were used both in 1997 and in 1998 by the opponents of the Italian initiative, as well as the counter-arguments with which the Italian delegation, both in its interventions at the Commission and in its bilateral lobbying in favour of the resolution, supported its stand.

Relativism

In the years after the fall of the Berlin Wall and the demise of Soviet communism we have witnessed an open ideological challenge to the universality of human rights, one consisting in the claim that the radical diversity of cultural traditions, religions, and social customs makes it arbitrary to identify (and impose) common standards in matters of human rights. The human rights debate – and controversy – has thus shifted from an east-west to a north-south dimension, and has been associated, on the part of many countries of the south, with denunciations of "cultural imperialism" and denial of the equal dignity of all peoples and all cultures.

It is not surprising that the issue of the death penalty should be addressed by retentionist countries in a relativist mode, and it is significant to note that the two groups, that is Asian and Islamic countries, that held the forefront, especially at the 53rd Session of the Commission, in the battle against the Italian resolution, are the most vocal and most articulate in developing the theme of relativism in all matters pertaining to human rights. Even more specifically, if we try to identify one state in 1997 as playing a leadership role in the retentionist camp, we clearly come up with Singapore, probably the most articulate and the earliest proponent of the relativist approach.

All these countries included in their arguments the complaint that the resolution proposed by Italy constituted an inadmissible attempt, on a matter as delicate as that of capital punishment, to impose views that were culturally specific and did not show sufficient respect for other traditions, also (this especially as far as the Islamic countries are concerned) of a religious nature.

The Italian delegation gave special attention to this latter objection, in particular in the light of its systematic striving for a non-confrontational approach. In doing so, it divided the matter of contention into two distinct aspects, reflecting the dual nature of the resolution. As far as the call to respect existing international obligations relating to the limitations and the conditions of application of the death penalty, it could not but state – and it did so – that existing norms cannot be eluded by making reference to different cultural traditions; cultural specificities are totally irrelevant in matters of compliance with international obligations. As for the gradual abolitionist approach, the anti-relativist rebuttal of the Italian delegation was couched in respectful, but firm language. The following quote from a 23 March 1998 intervention by the Italian delegate may suffice to give an idea of this approach:

"Some of our interlocutors have maintained that our initiative touches upon a matter, capital punishment, which has a direct connection with religious principles that no one should challenge or question. We think it is extremely important to dispel this misunderstanding. In no way would Italy, a country which has a deep respect for all religions, conceive of expressing critical judgments on any religious faith. Our starting point is definitely not one that aims at building walls or deepening cultural divides, quite the opposite. In this, as well as in any other aspect of the human rights debate, we feel on the contrary that our task is to find what we all have in common, after recognising with respect all our cultural differences. And the way we approach the issue of the death penalty is indeed on the basis of concepts which are common to all religions: the sanctity of human life, the value of human dignity, the precept of mercy, the gift of compassion. The fact that historically these principles have been applied in different degrees in different parts of the world certainly does not justify their appropriation by any one religion, nor, conversely, can their rejection be attributed to the precept of any religion."

Continuing this line of thought, it would be easy to object to the proponents of the "Asian values" thesis especially as far as the issue of capital punishment is concerned where, for instance, a major component of Asian spirituality is Buddhism, characterised by a radical, indiscriminate, respect for all life.[1] Or that, as Amartya Sen has clearly shown, the Hindu tradition comprises highly humane, non-repressive features that go against the simplistic caricature of "authoritarian Asian values."[2]

Sovereignty

Another argument utilised by opponents of the resolution was much wider in scope and potentially more effective than the relativist objection; I am referring to the argument of sovereignty.[3] Here, indeed, not only do we

---

1. At the 53rd Session of the CHR, Nepal broke ranks with the other Asians in order to affirm its different views on the issue and voted in favour of the resolution.
2. Amartya Sen (1997), *Human Rights and Asian Values*, (Sixteenth Morgenthau Memorial Lecture on Ethics and Foreign Policy), (New York: Carnegie Council on Ethics and International Affairs).
3. It must be recalled that in 1997 the most dangerous challenge to the resolution came from an amendment reaffirming "the sovereign right of states to determine the legal system appropriate to their societies".

touch upon the very core of the issue of the death penalty, but we enter the highly charged field of the relations between the state and the individual. "Sovereignty", in this context, is used in two different meanings: non-subjection to an external jurisdiction (*superiorem non recognoscens*), and uncontrolled power of the state over its own citizens. It is remarkable that, when dealing with the issue of capital punishment, the arguments used by retentionist countries go back to absolute concepts that do not seem any longer tenable in the light of the legal and even cultural evolution that has taken place since the birth of the nation-state system and the elaboration of theories on its essence and prerogatives. And, more specifically, in the light of the half century of existence of the United Nations.

Sovereignty of nation-states is still, of course, the basic foundation of the international system. And yet, several qualifications are in order:

- Sovereignty cannot be a pretext for the non-compliance with existing international norms.
- After the 1993 Vienna World Conference on Human Rights no state can pretend to declare human rights "off limits" to all external concern. The Vienna Declaration, on the contrary, specifies that "the promotion and protection of all human rights is the legitimate concern of the international community."
- As far as human life is concerned, in particular, it does not seem any longer tenable to maintain that the state has an unchallenged, uncontrolled right of life and death over its own citizens (the *jus vitae ac necis* that the paterfamilias had under Roman law). If it were so, the right to life proclaimed in a plurality of United Nations' texts as the very foundation of the entire human rights discourse would be bereft of all significance. As the Italian delegation said at the 54th Session of the Commission on Human Rights, it would be arbitrary to say that the death penalty today is illegal under international law, but it would be just as arbitrary to defend the notion that matters relating to the application of the death penalty fall invariably outside the scope of international law.

The present Secretary General of the United Nations, Kofi Annan, has addressed this basic conceptual aspect with all the caution needed, but all the clarity necessary. Writing in the *International Herald Tribune*, he has rebutted the idea that the internal nature of a conflict disqualifies the United Nations from dealing with it: "Can this be right? The United Nations' Charter, after all, was issued in the name of 'the people', not the governments, of the United Nations. Its aim is not only to preserve international peace – vitally important though that is – but also 'to re-affirm faith in fundamental human rights, in the dignity and worth of the human person.' The charter protects the sovereignty of peoples. It was never meant as a license for governments to trample on human rights and human dignity."[1] True, Annan writes here about internal conflicts, but his arguments are clearly applicable to all that pertains to "the dignity and worth of the human person", starting from the most basic issue of all: that of life or death.

Deterrence

While the previous two arguments are basically of an ideological nature, the argument concerning the need to use the death penalty in order to protect society is pragmatic, and as such can benefit from a wider margin of acceptance even among less militant retentionists. The concern for the spread of criminality is a real one in many, if not most countries, so that the idea of depriving the state of the ultimate tool of punishment (and thus, allegedly, of deterrence) strikes many as being a dangerous, if not irresponsible one. Again, a quote from an intervention by the Italian delegation can give an idea of the arguments that were used by Italy as well as by other supporters of the resolution:

> "The argument of the presumed deterrent effect of the death penalty is used especially by the representatives of countries in which crime, often organised crime, threatens the peace and security of citizens in an alarming and destabilising way. We recognise the good faith of those who have this reaction to such evident social evils and threats, but we would like to stress that criminologists and statisticians have not established a self-evident connection between the application of the death penalty and the decrease of violent crime, especially murder. A sounder, more factual, correlation seems to exist, on the contrary, between the certainty of punishment (jail sentences) and the decrease of crimes in general; the real deterrent is not the level of the punishment, but its inevitability. And let me say finally, on this point, that a glance at the map of capital punishment would justify the impression of a correlation which is diametrically opposed to what is imagined by those who speak of the death penalty as a deterrent; the places which register more executions are the same that register more murders."

Those who are in favour of retaining capital punishment frequently use the argument that death administered by the state substitutes and pre-empts revenge killing, a socially disruptive event. It is an argument that can be challenged, if one just thinks of episodes such as the delegation of relatives of the victim (in Taliban-controlled areas of Afghanistan) to the actual act of execution of a death sentence pronounced by a tribunal or (a less extreme, but still revealing fact) as the presence, in some countries, of the relatives of

---

1. Kofi A. Annan (1998), "The United Nations should intervene before force is needed," *International Herald Tribune*, 27-28 June.

the victim at the execution of the murderer. This is what the Italian delega-tion had in mind when it defined capital punishment as "an act which inevitably lies on the border between justice and revenge".[1]

Finally, a moral argument used by moderate retentionists has been the classical one of self-defence, a concept that is universally recognised as supplying an unchallengeable moral and legal justification for the use of even lethal violence. This argument lies at the root of the, albeit most limited, admission of the pos-sibility of the death penalty contained in the latest version of the Roman Catholic catechism (1997): the text states that the cases of "absolute necessity of the suppression of the culprit are now very rare, if not totally non-existent", but it recalls that the traditional teachings of the Church do not rule out capital punishment "if this were to be the only possible way to effectively defend human lives against an unjust aggressor".[2] Suffice it to say, here, that the argu-ment is basically flawed since self-defence has an intrinsically preventive func-tion (avoiding unjust harm) and is not applicable *post factum*, so that "self-defence" is improperly used in this context. It seems interesting to note that this line of thought inspired the Statement on Capital Punishment approved in 1980 by United States Catholic bishops who, in a clearly abolitionist document, ("We believe that in the conditions of contemporary American society, the legitimate purposes of punishment do not justify the imposition of the death penalty.") stated in particular that "both in its nature as a legal penalty and in its practical consequences, capital punishment is different from the taking of life in legiti-mate self-defence or in defence of society."[3] His Holiness, Jean Paul XXIII has gone even further in expressing himself in favour of abolition. In a recent speech in Mexico he states "There must be an end to the unnecessary recourse to the death penalty!", and again in St Louis he says:

> "the new evangelisation calls for followers of Christ who are uncondi-tionally pro-life; who will proclaim, celebrate and serve the Gospel of life in every situation. A sign of hope is the increasing recognition that the dignity of human life must never be taken away... I renew the appeal I made most recently at Christmas for a consensus to end the death penal-ty, which is both cruel and unnecessary."

These strong personal statements of the Pope against the death penalty thus point in the direction of a more explicit Roman Catholic Church stand on the issue.

---

1. In the same spirit, in a May 1998 lecture at the *Cercle Condorcet* in Geneva, the Vice-President of the Swiss Federal Council, Madame Ruth Dreifuss, said some very strong words on the death penalty, *"cette dérive de la vengeance, cette contamination de la violence."*
2. *Catechismus Catholicae Ecclesiae* (Citta' del Vaticano: Libreria Editrice Vaticana, 1997), p. 579.
3. The text can be found on the Internet at: www.pbs.org/wgbh/pages/frontline/angel/pro-con/bishopstate.html.

Conclusions

If this chapter concentrates on the 53rd and the 54th Sessions of the Commission on Human Rights (and on the Italian initiative – one, let us say, of "creeping abolitionism") it is not because the author believes that the resolutions approved in Geneva in 1997 and 1998 are definitive, historical events. Quite the contrary, the debate that took place at and around the Commission reveals that the march toward abolition will be a long and difficult one.

And yet those events in Geneva, though far from being definitive, point to trends that look comforting and promising to abolitionist eyes. That is, beyond the mere counting of votes, the different tenor of the debates and the difference of those countries' votes between 1997 and 1998 deserves to be noted.

Most significant was the fact that the attempt to "amend the resolution to death" that seriously threatened to wreck the initiative in 1997 was not renewed in 1998, when opponents (basically Asian and Islamic, with a few African states – but not the United States) drafted a common statement, in the form of a letter to the chairman of the Commission, expressing reservations on the resolution that were of a substantially moderate – one could say, defensive and rearguard – nature supported by both relativist and sovereignty arguments. This reflects a much less militant opposition on the part of Asian and Islamic countries, revealed by the fact that at the end it was the United States' delegation that had to take the leadership of the retentionist camp and to ask (after some meaningful seconds of silence when the chairman asked if the resolution could pass on the basis of consensus) for a vote on the resolution. In both the 1997 and 1998 sessions the United States' delegation conducted a very intense campaign against the Italian initiative, using the following arguments:

- the resolution is a departure from the established international consensus on capital punishment, since in the past resolutions approved in the United Nations context have so far only condemned arbitrariness and discrimination in the application of the death penalty, as well as summary executions;
- at present there is, on the contrary, no international consensus on whether capital punishment should be imposed or not, and a majority of countries have laws permitting capital punishment for the most serious crimes;
- international law does not prohibit capital punishment, and offers no basis for any call for its abolition;
- the Italian-sponsored resolution ignores the rights of states to impose capital punishment in accordance with international norms and safeguards.

Thus the basic purpose of the resolution seems to be attained; while recalling existing limitations, it contributed to transplanting the seed of abolitionism (that in a European context has grown into a sturdy and fruit-laden tree) into a global, United Nations framework.

One can add that whatever the facts and arguments on present-day norms, on United Nations mandates, on legitimate questioning of the way a state deals with its own citizens, it cannot be demanded of those who oppose the death penalty that, while duly respecting the existing rules of the game, they stop advocating, and promoting, a radical eventual outcome: total abolition. The resolutions that were approved at the sessions of the Commission on Human Rights in 1997 and 1998, and the interventions of their supporters leave no doubt that the more immediate regulatory and restrictive aim (including, especially in the 1998 resolution, the explicit focus on a moratorium) is not in contradiction with the aim of total abolition.

And it can no longer be dismissed as quixotic to imagine (and hope) that one day the death penalty will be considered inadmissible both in terms of a universal ethos and cogent international norms. In other words, it will go the way ancient institutions such as slavery or torture went – after being challenged only by dissident individuals or by minority views and long defended by mainstream thought and conventional wisdom (with reference to cultural and even religious traditions)[1] and an insistence on the fact that those institutions were "perfectly legal", stressing paramount social needs.

More specifically, and beyond the possibility of a wider acceptance of normative texts such as the Second Optional Protocol to the Covenant on Civil and Political Rights, we can imagine a time when the prohibition of the death penalty will become a part of customary international law, such as in the case of genocide, slavery, torture.[2]

Let us conclude, however, with a note of caution. The optimistic scenario sketched above is by no means an automatic, foregone outcome of present-

---

1. In the framework of late eighteenth century debate on slavery, one finds even an anti-abolitionist pamphlet with the title *Scriptural Researches on the Licitness of the Slave Trade*: quoted in Hugh Thomas, *The Slave Trade* (1997), New York; Simon and Schuster, p. 509. The nineteenth century political, ideological and legal confrontation on the slave trade is especially relevant in our context, since it is an evident case of divergence between moral belief and international legality – a divergence that tends, however, to be eventually bridged with the introduction of new legal norms. See Alfred P. Rubin (1997), *Ethics and Authority in International Law*. Cambridge University Press, in particular the chapter "The Impact of Reality on Theory," pp. 87-137.
2. The yearly supplement to the previous five-year reports on the death penalty – the yearly report is a follow-up that is mandated by Resolution 1997/12 – reveals that abolitionism is slowly gaining ground, going from 58 to 61 fully abolitionist countries, with 90 countries, however, still in the retentionist category. See E/CN.4/ 1998/82.

day debates and controversy, and though one can be confident in the eventual point of arrival, the pace of this evolution is not pre-determined, nor are temporary stagnation or even regression to be ruled out.

On the contrary, if we look at the characteristics of present-day society we see more than one reason for concern that some of those characteristics might negatively impact on the abolitionist cause. We are referring to globalisation, and this from a double perspective.

In the first place, one of the most distinctive characteristics of globalisation is the fact that it brings about proximity but not homogeneity, or at least it brings about proximity well before any possible homogenising effect on the working of a global economic system. But it goes without saying that proximity plus difference spells social tension, conflict, and that it especially entails a feeling of insecurity on the part of those (the "haves") who are suddenly confronted with the threatening contiguity of the once-distant "have nots". Statistics are not ambiguous, in so far as they reveal the high percentage of crime that can be attributed to this "non-homogeneous proximity".

Secondly, the generalised trend toward "less government" that characterises our increasingly globalised world entails demonstrable benefits in terms of economic dynamism, de-bureaucratisation, individual initiative. Yet, in countries where the rule of law is weaker, the political and economic shrinking of the state has left an open door to powerful and uncontrolled organised crime, that is to the often ferocious combination of illegal economic power and a capacity to administer personal violence.

Both threats are serious and disconcerting, and citizens in their fear can become deaf to humanity and decency, and cling to (or even revert to) the ancient illusion that administering legal death is the best way to ensure social tranquillity and protection.

This is why on a global level the abolitionist cause is actually only taking its first steps. Therefore it will be important in the next few years to consolidate the results achieved in Geneva (and carry them over, successfully, to the United Nations General Assembly) while continuing within civil society[1] a cultural and moral debate that goes beyond – but, let me assure readers, lies behind – the diplomatic struggle conducted by abolitionists. Not only Italy, not only Europe, but a growing number of countries belonging to different

---

1. The campaign for the abolition of capital punishment has seen, in Italy and elsewhere, a strong and very fruitful "division of roles" between government representatives and NGOs, each operating in different modes and with different languages, but clearly with a common goal.

regions share a common conviction in the need to abolish this terrible exception to the most essential of all human rights: the right to life.

*The views expressed in this text are exclusively those of the author and
should not be interpreted as reflecting official analyses of the Italian
Government.*

8. THE ABOLITION OF THE DEATH PENALTY IN FRANCE

Michel Forst, Director, Amnesty International, France

Until the end of the eighteenth century, few people in France questioned the legitimacy of capital punishment. But when 26-year-old Cesare Beccaria published his treatise *Dei delletti et della pene* (*On Crimes and Punishments*) in 1764, ideas gradually began to change; a new era dawned in which debates began that would lead to the first abolitionist movement.

As the eighteenth century drew to a close, France debated the workings of its justice system. Without actually calling for abolition of the death penalty, Voltaire campaigned against the barbarity of executions and for improvements to the judicial system. The sentences in two criminal cases (those of Calas and the Chevalier de la Barre) provoked indignation amongst Enlightenment figures, intellectuals and even what is now known as public opinion.

"If I can prove that this punishment is neither useful nor necessary, I will have furthered the cause of humanity," wrote Beccaria. In much of Europe, and indeed the world, his work was a huge success and the debate on capital punishment was never to stop completely for the next two centuries.

In France, some political figures supported Beccaria's arguments, but others refuted them point by point. Voltaire, who had initially been dubious about the abolition of capital punishment, was won over in 1777, and other thinkers followed his lead. At the Constituent National Assembly, Louis-Michel de Saint Fargeau, rapporteur on the draft criminal code, made the first speech against the death penalty. He put forward alternative sentences, but his opponents won the day. After long discussions, the Constituent National Assembly noted in its minutes: "When the main question was put to the vote, the Assembly decided almost unanimously that the death penalty would not be repealed."

Robespierre, an unexpected supporter of abolition, was one of those who spoke. He set out to show "firstly, that the death penalty is essentially unjust and, secondly, that it is not the most dissuasive sentence and increases crime much more than it prevents it". Robespierre was never to put his principles into practice. Once in power, he lacked the political courage to impose his ideas and preferred to give effect to public opinion as expressed in the register of grievances of the 1789 Estates General: "the death penalty must be used … but in a less painful way".

In the spring of 1791, the Constituent National Assembly adopted a new Criminal Code with its never-to-be-forgotten Article 3: "Every condemned person shall be beheaded". It was at this point that an inventor came up with "a less painful way" of delivering the fatal blow, claiming that "the principle of equality" in death had finally become possible thanks to a newly invented improvement on the executioner's axe. Doctor Guillotin undertook to put the invention into practice: "I'll take your head off in the twinkling of an eye and you won't feel a thing". The machine was adopted and the guillotine used for the first time on 25 April 1792. Two centuries later, the same reasoning led the United States to introduce lethal injections – and other countries followed their example. In spite of Condorcet's entreaties, the convention sent the king and his family to the guillotine; the day after the sentence was passed, he unsuccessfully tabled a motion in favour of abolition.

According to some historians 1 373 heads rolled between 10 June 1794 and Robespierre's fall on 27 July. This was the apogee of the legal use of capital punishment in France. Revolutionary justice is said to have executed between thirty and forty thousand people. So much for Beccaria!

Nevertheless, the idea of abolition continued to advance. A few years later, in the Act of 4 Brumaire, year IV, the convention abolished capital punishment, but included a qualification that would prove its undoing: "from the date of publication of the general peace". In 1810, the Napoleonic Code put an end to this conditional abolition. Abolition would not be achieved step by step, it had to be total and without provisos.

After the Consulate and the Empire, executions continued under the Restoration. The debate over the death penalty was re-opened in the nineteenth century with the publication of Victor Hugo's *Le dernier jour d'un condamné* (*The last day of a condemned man*). Respected academics, lawyers, and political and literary figures united in condemning a barbaric and pointless punishment but continued to be opposed on grounds of law and order: "If a state abolishes the death penalty, it runs the risk of having criminals from neighbouring states rush on to its territory". Alain Peyrefitte, the Justice Minister, re-used this argument in 1979.

In spite of all opposition, the abolitionist movement started by Beccaria continued to progress. In 1786, Grand-Duke Leopold of Tuscany promulgated a criminal code that completely abolished the death penalty. In 1794, the Pennsylvania Quakers asserted their abolitionist principles. In 1846, Michigan, later to become a state, was the first territory in the world to abolish the death penalty irrevocably for intentional homicide. In 1863, Venezuela became the first country to abolish it definitively for all crimes. Other countries went down the same path. The little Republic of San Marino abolished the death penalty for all crimes in 1865; it had already abolished it for ordinary crimes in 1848 and had not carried out a single execution since gaining independence in 1468, well before Beccaria's time. In many European countries, the death penalty fell into disuse. Monaco's last execution was carried out in 1847, Liechtenstein's in 1785, and Portugal's in 1849. In Africa, where the concept of abolition was still new, the Cape Verde Islands deserve mention: the last execution was carried out in 1835.

In France, dazzling orators demonstrated the futility of the death penalty in theory, yet progress towards abolition was as rare in legislative terms as in judicial practice. On 17 March 1838, Lamartine addressed the Chamber of Deputies in support of abolition, affirming that the death penalty had become ineffective and harmful in a developed society. Ten years were to pass before some small progress was achieved: in an 1848 decree, confirmed by the Second Empire on 15 June 1853, the provisional government of the Second Republic abolished the death penalty for political crimes. Political offences had still to be defined, France has still not defined them to this day.

Over the years, members of parliament have frequently demanded the abolition of the death penalty, but always without success, until the first years of Armand Fallières' presidency. Elected in January 1906, this confirmed abolitionist had the opportunity to leave a lasting mark on his era. His predecessor, Emile Loubet, had already made wide use of his prerogative of mercy and expressed his horror at the death penalty. Armand Fallières immediately put the abolition debate on the agenda. Decisions were taken. The Budget Committee of the Chamber of Deputies voted to end funding to maintain the guillotine and pay the executioner. Aristide Briand, Minister of Justice in Clémenceau's government, submitted a bill for the abolition of the death penalty to the Chamber. This bill, tabled in 1906, was not debated in the Assembly until 8 December 1908. Spiritedly presented by the Minister for Justice, it was supported by the politicians Jean Jaurès and Deschanel, and eloquently opposed by the intellectual Maurice Barrès. When it was put to the vote, 333 were in favour of maintaining the death penalty, 201 were against.

There was a simple explanation for this rejection – a little girl had been murdered in the meantime. The accused's trial began on 23 July 1907. Before the court had delivered its verdict, a daily newspaper, *Le Petit Parisien*, condemned the defendant. The press made as much mileage as possible out of this dreadful story. As soon as the death penalty had been handed down, before the Assembly's vote, despite the press and a large part of public opinion, Armand Fallières remained faithful to his convictions and reprieved the condemned man on 13 September. The press went wild and condemned his decision. At the end of September, *Le Petit Parisien* launched what it termed a "referendum", complete with financial incentives, which it then relaunched in October so as to obtain more replies. The results were published on 5 November; almost 77% of respondents were in favour of the death penalty being carried out.

The act maintaining the death penalty was therefore adopted. After a three-year interval, executions were resumed: 223 persons were executed between 1906 and 1929, and 89 between 1934 and 1938.

A public execution in 1939 might have swayed public opinion, but it was not to be. Versailles, 16 June: the guillotine was badly set up, and the lunette and blade were defective. The execution was a particularly dreadful example, and once again, the spectators came running, as though going to a fair. As *Paris Match* reported: "The crowd was not deterred", and the newspapers published many photographs. However, as a result of the "incidents" that had marred the execution, the government held an extraordinary meeting and, in a decree of 25 June, abolished the public nature of executions. Executions have not taken place in public since.

The guillotine and specialised courts were used under the German occupation. War-torn Europe saw an upsurge in the use of capital punishment. In France, Marshal Pétain broke with an almost century-old tradition when he sent five women to the guillotine. President Auriol continued this practice in 1947 and 1949 by refusing to reprieve two women convicted of killing their husbands.

Abolitionists were a tiny minority, or unable to make their voices heard. There was still a long way to go from the guillotine to abolition.

Executions continued at the rate of one to four a year. Albert Camus and Alfred Koestler published *Réflexion sur la guillotine* (*Reflections on the Guillotine*), an eloquent treatise against the death penalty. A few courageous politicians continued to table private member's bills to abolish the death penalty, with cross-party support. None of these reached the floor of the Chamber.

George Pompidou's arrival at the Elysée gave the abolitionists some hope. On 15 June 1969, he reprieved the six prisoners sentenced to death since the beginning of his presidency. The polls vindicated his decision: in May, 39% of French people were in favour of the death penalty, 50% were opposed, and 11% were "don't knows". In October, a new poll showed 33% for capital punishment, 58% against, and 9% undecided.

However, public opinion is a fickle thing, and the National Assembly was not yet amenable: private member's bills continued to be rejected, and a fresh news story reversed the poll findings.

On 21 September 1971 two prisoners took a nurse and a warder hostage in one of France's strictest prisons. One of the men had already been sentenced to life imprisonment for murder, the other to twenty years' imprisonment for aggravated theft and assault. Dramatic negotiations took place between the hostage-takers and the prison administration, which refused to meet their demands. The building was stormed, and the two hostages were found with their throats slit.

The prison staff reacted furiously. Guards attempted to overturn the vehicle carrying the prisoners to the Paris region, and several trade unions organised a national day of protest. Statement after statement was issued. Public opinion became ever more enraged. As the prison van passed, shouting crowds demanded the prisoners' heads

When the trial opened, some of the press were already speculating on the prisoners' fate. Newspapers, radio and television covered the proceedings. Once the verdict had been made public, much of the press greeted the double death sentence with a certain satisfaction: on 30 June 1972, the *Parisien Libéré* headlined with "Death sentence for cut-throats Buffet and Bontems". The court delivered this verdict on the same day that the United States Supreme Court declared the death penalty "unconstitutional".

French public opinion swung: in September, 53% were in favour of the death penalty, 39% against and 8% had no opinion.

Would Pompidou still grant a reprieve? He was in no hurry to decide. Rightly or wrongly, he was believed to be hostile to the death penalty. Why was he taking so long to make his decision known? While everyone wondered, *France Soir* published the results of a new poll showing that 63% of French people were in favour of the death penalty.

Pompidou refused to reprieve the men and justice took its course. Buffet and Bontems were executed on 29 November 1972.

Michel Foucault, a distinguished sociologist, wrote in a weekly paper:

> "Once again, the prison administration had prevailed over the justice system. Before the trial, and before any reprieve, it demanded its 'justice' and got its way. An institution that should have no other concern but unemotionally to carry out sentences, which it is for others to decide, gauge and supervise, has openly demanded, and has been accorded, the right to punish. We know what pressure has been brought to bear by the prison warders' unions to obtain this double execution. It has set itself up as a power in the land, and the head of state has just given his agreement."

Thus, to quote Mr Crauste, a member of Claude Buffet's defence team: "this decision by the head of state is particularly regrettable... at one stroke, it has set our criminal justice system back a hundred years." In the same year, President Pompidou reprieved Mohamed Libdiri, who had been convicted of murdering a taxi driver.

Foreign reaction to the double execution of the prisoners was highly critical; a liberal Swedish paper wrote "29 November 1972 is a shameful day for French officialdom, which often claims to set an example for enlightened modern states". Sweden abolished the death penalty that same year.

Three years later, a new drama unfolded; a young girl was abducted on 3 June 1974 and her body found two days later. Christian Ranucci, who had just turned twenty, was arrested, tried and sentenced to death after a muddled investigation. He was guillotined in a courtyard of Marseilles' Baumettes prison on 28 July 1976. His last words to his lawyers were "Clear my name". Since then, all attempts to re-open the case have been turned down. As in many countries, the French justice system rarely recognises its mistakes, and the defendant is not always given the benefit of the doubt. Giscard d'Estaing, who could have granted a reprieve, refused.

While abolition was gaining ground across Europe, the history of the guillotine and the death penalty was not yet over in France.

A memorable trial – that of Patrick Henri – began on 18 January 1977. One weekly newspaper told the story under the headline "Trial of a guillotined man". The defendant seemed undefendable. His child victim had been abducted in the hope of obtaining a ransom from the parents, first locked up in a hotel room and then killed. Before his arrest Henri had said "I am in favour of the death penalty for people who pick on children".

Before Henri's arrest, during the nearly three-week-long search, one public pronouncement followed another. Eschewing the discretion appropriate to their positions, the Minister for Justice, the Minister of the Interior and the

Minister for Infrastructure (mayor of the town where the drama unfolded) demanded at least "an exceptional punishment", or went so far as to call for the death penalty. The case took an emotional turn and the media helped to dramatise it further. It became difficult to find a defence lawyer for this young man, accused of the horrendous murder of a child. Mr Bocquillon, Chairman of the Bar, and then Robert Badinter agreed to "weigh on the conscience of the jury" and defend Patrick Henri. By the time the trial started, the public had already reached their verdict.

After a three day trial and two hours of deliberation, the jury returned its verdict: Patrick Henri was sentenced to life imprisonment. France was astonished. The press refrained from committing itself, voicing its disapproval only by reporting the crowd's expressions of discontent, but Le Monde's special correspondent concluded his column on a hopeful note: "History will perhaps pay tribute to these nine ordinary French people who, as the day broke, were the first to have the courage to abolish the death penalty."

This was 21 January 1977. The United States had just ended its unofficial moratorium on executions, and Gary Gilmore, who wanted to die, had faced the firing squad in Utah on 17 January.

That year, Amnesty International held a conference in Stockholm, preceded by six preparatory seminars in Paris, Hamburg, New York, Colombo, Ibadan and Port of Spain. The conference highlighted the fact that not only was capital punishment used in a great many cases for political ends, but that it was by its nature a political instrument. The conference ended with the adoption of a declaration expressing Amnesty International's position on the death penalty and an action programme against capital punishment. At the close of the Stockholm conference, Robert Badinter, who had been a key contributor, said "Amnesty International's greatest merit is that it does not simply treat the death penalty as though it were a separate issue that could be resolved by abolition, without also mounting a constant and vigorous defence against attacks on fundamental human rights, of which the right to life is but the first."

In France too, we had seen the death penalty used as a "political argument" for attracting votes. However, in the presidential campaign that took place a few years later, it became clear that it was not wise to choose political positions on the basis of opinion polls. However, we have not yet reached that stage in our story.

Between 1978 and the 1981 presidential election, the parliamentary debate was pushed forward by a "study group for abolition", set up by a cross-party group of deputies in the National Assembly. Abolitionist organisations, led by all the members of the French section of Amnesty International, lobbied to encourage politicians, deputies, senators, and actual or potential presidential candidates to support abolition.

In October 1978, the parliamentary group attempted to introduce abolition by ending the budgetary allocations to pay the executioner and maintain the guillotine. This was not a new idea, since the same tactic had been used in 1906.

Finally, in 1979, several deputies close to the government, including Pierre Bas, Philippe Séguin and Bernard Stasi, tabled a private member's bill on abolition, forcing Alain Payrefitte, the Justice Minister, to hold a debate. On 15 June, the *Commission des Lois* voted for abolition of the death penalty, but the Justice Minister stated that "the time has not yet come". The debate was entered on the June programme but no vote was taken. On 26 June Alain Peyrefitte made a speech to the National Assembly advocating the abolition of the death penalty, but without actually abolishing it!

Following Christian Ranucci's death, President Giscard d'Estaing refused to reprieve condemned men on two further occasions. As of May 1999 Hamida Djandoubi was the last person to be beheaded in France, on 10 September 1977.

The electoral campaign at the end of Valéry Giscard d'Estaing's presidency was finally the opportunity for a major debate on the death penalty, and its abolition became a campaign issue.

On 4 November 1980, by becoming a state party to the International Covenant on Civil and Political Rights, France had undertaken to stop applying the death penalty to persons aged below 18 years at the time of the crime, and to pregnant women. The ratification, which entered into force on 29 January 1981, was published in the Official Gazette on 1 February 1981.

However, the story was to take one last twist. On 5 November 1980, another draft amendment to abolish funding for the costs of capital punishment was rejected. In 1980, when thirteen European states had already abolished the death penalty, Valéry Giscard d'Estaing, who was seeking re-election, said "I have a profound distaste for the death penalty…". Further, "I believe that such a change can only take place in a peaceable society whose members are confident about their safety. And as long as this assurance is not felt, it (abolition) would go against the deepest sensibilities of the French people". One is reminded of the convention, which abolished the death penalty "from the date of publication of the general peace". To go against the deepest sensibilities of the French people or to go against the polls? That was the question, as opinion polls were still being conducted, and most French people were opposed to abolition.

Nevertheless, during *Cartes sur la table*, a French television programme on the presidential election campaign, the candidate François Mitterrand spelled out his convictions:

> "As with the other issues, I will not hide my views on the death penalty. And I have no intention of going to the country in this race and pretending to be something that I am not. In my innermost conscience, like the churches, the Catholic church, the Reformed churches, Judaism, and all the important national and international humanitarian associations, in my heart of hearts, I am opposed to the death penalty... I am standing for the presidency of the French Republic, and in asking for a majority of French people's votes, I do not hide what I think. I say what I think, what I hold to, what I believe in, and what my spiritual beliefs and concern for civilisation are based on: I am not in favour of the death penalty."

Elections are not won by scrutinising opinion polls, but by proposing values that correspond to beliefs. This was proved on 10 May 1981, when François Mitterrand was elected President of the Republic.

Decisions followed quickly. As President, François Mitterrand decided to commute a death sentence handed down on 28 October 1980. This was the case of Philippe Maurice, described by the press as "a hooligan, cop-killer and hostage-taker", whose PhD dissertation, written in prison, was to obtain a distinction and the academic jury's congratulations fourteen years later. But the death penalty still existed in France: in May 1981, three people were sentenced to death.

While the European Parliament, meeting in Strasbourg, adopted several resolutions concerning abolition on 18 June 1981, Robert Badinter, the new Minister for Justice for France, announced the proposed abolition of the death penalty, among other measures, at a press conference on 9 July.

On 26 August the French Cabinet proposed a bill abolishing the death penalty, which was then tabled by Robert Badinter on 31 August. The French Parliament met in extraordinary session and the debates began on 8 September. The French, who had elected François Mitterrand for his new ideas, remained for the most part in favour of the death penalty; a poll by Sofres for *Le Figaro* on 8 and 10 September revealed that 62% of the population were in favour of maintaining the guillotine. Would our deputies have the courage to defend republican values?

On 17 September, the National Assembly began to debate the bill to abolish the death penalty. It was a historic moment for France when at 5 p.m. Robert Badinter, the Minister for Justice, took the floor and made a solemn speech which would remain in the historic annals of the Chamber:

> "President, Deputies, I am honoured, on behalf of the government of the Republic, to ask the National Assembly to vote for the abolition of the death penalty in France.
>
> At this time, and I know you are all aware of its significance for our justice system and for ourselves, I would like first of all to thank (…) all those who, whatever their political persuasion, have worked in recent years, particularly within the previous *Commissions des Lois*, to ensure that abolition was introduced, long before the major political change that we are now experiencing…
>
> This like-minded thinking across political divides shows that the debate beginning here today is primarily one of conscience and the choice each of you makes will be a personal commitment…
>
> … Tomorrow, thanks to you, the French justice system will no longer be a system that kills. Tomorrow, through your efforts, the collective shame of furtive dawn executions under a black canopy will be put to an end in French prisons. Tomorrow, the bloody pages in the history of our justice system will be turned.
>
> At this time more than any other, I have the feeling of fulfilling my ministry, in the ancient, noble sense – the most noble possible – of 'service'. Tomorrow, you will vote for the abolition of the death penalty. French deputies, I thank you from the bottom of my heart."

The vote was taken on 18 September, and its result was unequivocal. The only question had been how large the majority would be. Article 1, abolishing the death penalty, was adopted by 369 votes to 113. The bill itself was adopted by 363 votes to 117.

Some concerns remained about how the Senate would vote. After debate, the Senate definitively adopted the bill abolishing the death penalty on 30 September 1981, by 160 votes to 126.

France had thus finally abolished the death penalty for all crimes, both civilian and military, by Act No. 81-908 of 9 October 1981, which entered into force on the following day. The first article stated that "The death penalty is abolished". The six French prisoners already sentenced to death were reprieved.

Three years later, the number of French people in favour of abolition was slightly higher than those who regretted its abolition; 49% to 46%, according to an opinion poll carried out by IFRES. For any head of state, however, it is advisable to add the weight of international law to abolition at national level. An international obligation makes it impossible to restore capital punishment and remains the best method of resisting pressure and creating an obstacle that will prevent any hasty return to the previous situation.

By ratifying the first international instrument on abolition of the death penalty, Protocol No. 6 to the Convention for the Protection of Human Rights and Fundamental Freedoms, France thus undertook, by international agreement, not to reintroduce the death penalty in peacetime, save by derogation from the Protocol in accordance with the terms of Article 65 of the European Convention. The ratification was recorded at the Council of Europe on 17 February 1986.

Today, the death penalty has been abolished in most of Europe. The Parliamentary Assembly of the Council of Europe adopted Resolution 1097 of 28 June 1996, confirming its opposition to the death penalty, and Resolution 1302 calling on the Committee of Ministers to consider without further delay (with a view to drawing up a new protocol) the proposal recommending abolition of the death penalty under all circumstances. On 12 June 1997, the European Parliament itself adopted a resolution whereby in paragraph 6 it "proposes that candidate countries for accession to the Council of Europe should undertake to sign and ratify the second optional Protocol to the International Covenant on Civil and Political Rights as a condition of membership". In April 1998, for the second year in a row, the United Nations Commission on Human Rights adopted a resolution in favour of a universal moratorium on executions. Now that the number of abolitionist states in the world is greater than the number of states that continue to execute, what can be said about French public opinion?

If the opinion polls are to be believed, after more than twenty years without an execution, the majority of the French public are still not convinced. Yet is this a well-informed opinion, is there a thorough understanding of the facts and the risks involved in the death penalty? Finally, what value and significance should be given to opinion polls?

To take a recent example: two institutes polled the French population on the same date. One announced "54% of those questioned said that they did not wish the death penalty to be restored", but the other stated "50% are in favour of the death penalty and 46% against". What can be deduced from these figures? The majority of French people are thus in favour of the death penalty but do not want it to be restored. Or does this difference reflect the way in which the questions were worded? Without accusing the research institutes of dishonesty, do their questions not correspond – consciously or unconsciously – to the expectations of the research company's client? The first question in the IFOB poll[1] was "Are you in favour of restoring the death penalty?". The BVA's second question asked "Are you in favour of the death penalty?".

Amnesty International believes that respect for life and the human rights that protect it must never depend on public opinion, but that those responsible for policy in this area have a duty to ensure that the public is well-informed. Some research suggests that attitudes to the death penalty may change if the facts are better known. Repeated research over a number of years has shown that although the decision to abolish the death penalty may initially offend, abolition is eventually accepted.

Nowadays, although abolitionists are still in the minority, their ideas have nevertheless gained ground. The more the real facts about the death penalty are known, the more people will fight to abolish forever this violation of human rights. Progress has been made, and it must be continued until we have created a world in which there will be no more executions.

After Europe, which has now almost entirely abolished the death penalty, we must, together with the Council of Europe and the United Nations, build a world in which the death penalty is completely illegal.

In working towards this goal, the members of Amnesty International identify with this advice from Robert Badinter, given at a Council of Europe colloquy in April 1989: "What we need in human rights, even more than speeches and colloquies, is action and commitment; even more than philosophers, lawyers or ministers, we need activists."

---

1. IFOB and BVA are opinion poll institutes.

9. THE DEATH PENALTY IN SLOVAKIA

JUDr. Robert Fico, CSc., Ministry of Justice of Slovakia

A brief historical background

The death penalty has been used since time immemorial in the territory of the present-day Slovakia. The first codified criminal codes, such as the *Constitutio Criminalis Josephina* of 1707 or *Constitutio Criminalis Thereziana* of 1768 provided for a broad use of capital punishment typically performed with extraordinary cruelty. Therefore it is quite surprising to find a brief period during late feudalism when the death penalty was abolished *de facto* and *de jure*, as set out in the *General Code of Crimes and Punishments* (*Všeobecny zákonník o zloèinoch a trestoch na ne*) of 1787 adopted during the reign of Joseph II. This became the legal framework for all criminal legislation in Slovakia until 1950. This law was significantly influenced by the humanistic ideals of Ceasare Beccaria's essay *On Crimes and Punishments* (*Dei deliti e delle pene*) of 1764, containing very cruel alternatives to the death penalty, such as dragging by a ship, etc. Emperor Joseph II closely followed Beccaria's ideas, and ordered by his secret decrees of 1781 and 1783 that every case involving the death penalty be submitted to him personally. Thus, he was able to grant pardon systematically to all such criminals. The only execution occurred in 1786. This abolitionist period was short, because soon after Joseph's death, Emperor Franz II issued a decree in 1796 by which the death penalty was restored.

Following the formation of the Czechoslovak Republic in 1918, dual laws of the Austrian and Hungarian monarchy became incorporated into the criminal system, so that until 1950, Slovakia was governed under laws different to those applied in the Czech territories. In Slovakia and the Carpathian Ruthenia, the Criminal Code on Crimes and Misdemeanours (*Trestný zákonník o zločinoch a prečinoch*) adopted as Legislative Enactment V of 1878 was in force between 1918 and 1950. Under this ancient Hungarian criminal law the death penalty was imposed only for cases of murder. Apart from the Criminal Code, there was a law of 1885 governing the operation of explosives, and the Legislative Enactment XIX of 1915 regulating military provisions, in which the death penalty was also included.

As published in the available sources, the total number of criminal offenders executed in the whole of Czechoslovakia between 1918 and 1933 was nine. Imposition of the death penalty was supported also by T.G. Masaryk (1850-1937), the first Czechoslovak President:

> "My argument in favour of the death penalty is not its deterring effect but moral expiation: taking someone's life is a wrong so dreadful that it can be reprieved by a suffering similarly dreadful ... I do believe and expect that it will be abolished as a result of a higher literacy and morals of the whole population, and consent of us all."

The tragic 1950s

While in other countries resistance to the death penalty grew after the second world war, the onset of communist power in Czechoslovakia in 1948 brought not only an excessive number of death sentences but also abuse of the death penalty for political reasons. Prior to the Criminal Code of 1950, the Act for the Protection of the Republic was passed in 1948, under which the death penalty was used for political offences, and was in practice used unjustifiably to physically liquidate political opposition. Under this law, between 1948 and 1950 the total number of death penalties imposed for political offences was ninety-nine, and sixteen for cases of murder.

The new Criminal Code in force for the whole of Czechoslovakia was adopted in 1950, also provided for the imposition of the death penalty for criminal and political offences (altogether twenty-five crimes were defined). The operation of the Criminal Code, until 1955 in particular, reflected the unhappy ideas of a permanently growing class struggle. Based on statistical data, there were 158 cases of the death penalty being imposed during the period 1951 to 1955. And the number of all cases involving the death penalty imposed for political delicts between 1948 and 1955 reached 257.

The tragic 1950s are occasionally used as a proof of miscarriage of justice. In the case of Czechoslovakia, this was not the traditional miscarriage of justice but intentional misuse of criminal law and of the death penalty for the physical liquidation of political opposition.

Partial admission of gross violation of the law by the police, public prosecutors and the courts in 1956 had some impact on the statutory regulation of the death penalty. Some of the definitions of crimes punishable by death, and imprisonment for life were abolished. The death penalty was attenuated by a sanction of twenty-five years' imprisonment. A duty of mandatory review of all death sentences by the Czechoslovak Supreme Court was introduced, and became a very important measure. Between 1962 and 1988, the Czechoslovak courts imposed 131 death sentences, 42 of which were quashed by the Czechoslovak Supreme Court.

The Criminal Code and Code of Criminal Procedure of 1961

The new codes of 1961 brought a new statutory regulation, which – except for several small changes – was in force until 1990, when the death penalty was abolished *de jure* and *de facto* in Czechoslovakia. In the 1961 measures, thirty-three crimes were defined, including political offences, for which the death penalty could be imposed. However, the death penalty was not the only punishment for the offences enumerated, and was, in any single case, a strictly controlled alternative to a term of imprisonment. To impose the death penalty it was not sufficient to satisfy the requirements of a crime defined as punishable by death. Other conditions had to be met; there had to be an extraordinary high degree of danger to society; the belief that the imposition of the death penalty was required for the effective protection of the community; or the belief in the absence of prospects of reform for the offender by a prison term up to fifteen years. There were three alternative criteria set to test the presence of an extraordinarily high degree of danger to society, namely: the extreme brutality of the commission of crime, the extreme wickedness of the intent and the degree of seriousness and irreparable consequences of the crime.

Because of a substantial difference between the sentence of up to fifteen years' imprisonment and the punishment by death, another punishment was introduced in 1973; imprisonment for not less than fifteen and not more than twenty-five years. The court could impose this punishment instead of the death penalty even where the criteria for the death penalty were met, provided the court thought that a long-term prison sentence would be adequate to satisfy the aim and purpose of punishment. The courts used this extraordinary term of imprisonment, and between 1973 and 1978 it was imposed on sixty-four offenders who might otherwise be executed. Some procedural guarantees should be mentioned here, by which the death penalty was forbidden in cases of pregnant women, or persons, who, at the time of the commission of the offence, had not attained the age of eighteen. A decision in the case of an offence punishable by death was always made by a trial court which had also an appellate jurisdiction, so that the appeal therefrom was to the Supreme Court of the Czech Republic or the Supreme Court of the Slovak Republic, as the case may be. In addition, each case was then mandatorily reviewed by the Federal Supreme Court of Czechoslovak Republic as mentioned above.

Analysis of the death penalty in Slovakia from 1970 to 1990

In this period, there were thirty-one convicted persons lawfully sentenced to death in Slovakia. From all cases mandatorily reviewed by the Supreme Court of the Czechoslovak Republic, twenty-one sentences were upheld by the Supreme Court, and sixteen persons were executed. For the sake of avoiding any possible misunderstanding, it should be noted again that the criminal codes were in force in the whole of Czechoslovakia, and that besides the Federal Supreme Court of the Czechoslovak Republic, there were also the Supreme Court of the Slovak Republic, and the Supreme Court of the Czech Republic.

The analysis focusing on the cases of actual executions supported by the appropriate court files afforded the following conclusions to be made:

- Fifteen criminals were executed for murder (double murder in eight cases), one person for attempted triple killing of policemen acting on duty.
- Although there were three alternative criteria fixed by law to establish the extraordinary high degree of danger to society, the courts based their decisions on two and even all three criteria at the same time. This further substantiates the conclusion that execution of the death penalty occurred only for brutal crimes committed with extraordinary cruelty and malignity.
- All the executed criminals were men, and none of them was a first-time offender. All criminals had a history of various serious crimes.
- The expert opinion of psychiatrists and sexologists in individual cases confirmed that the executed criminals were profoundly deviant. The crimes were mostly committed under the influence of intoxication by alcohol.
- There was a significant disparity between the number of offences punishable by death and the actual imposition of the penalty. Not only since 1970, but beginning in 1962, when the Criminal Code of 1961 came into effect, the death penalty was imposed only for extremely serious crimes of murder. There was no inclination to impose the death penalty for other offences defined in the Code and punishable by death.

In 1988, the existing provisions governing the death penalty and their application was surveyed in relation to the United Nations Economic and Social Council Resolution 1984/50 concerning the safeguards guaranteeing protection of the rights of those facing the death penalty. The Czechoslovak legislation and its practical application were fully in conformity with the requirements of this resolution.

Abolition of the death penalty de jure and de facto in 1990

The death penalty was abolished in Czechoslovakia *de jure* and *de facto* for both peace and wartime by the Amendment of the Criminal Code brought into effect as of 1 July 1990. Alongside the extraordinary sentence of imprisonment for fifteen to twenty-five years, the sentence of life imprisonment was reintroduced. The development was amply concluded with the adoption of the *Charter of Fundamental Rights and Freedoms of 9 January 1991*, under which "the death penalty shall be inadmissible" was provided by Article 6 paragraph 3. The same formulation was then transferred to Article 15 of the Constitution of the Slovak Republic in effect as of 1 October 1992. The division of the Czech and Slovak Federal Republic on 1 January 1993 had no impact on the legislation governing extraordinary punishments, as both independent countries used the same criminal laws.

The Czech and Slovak Federal Republic joined the Council of Europe on 18 March 1992, and this is also the date of ratification of Protocol No. 6 to the Convention for the Protection of Human Rights and Fundamental Freedoms. Following the break-up of the federal republic, the Slovak Republic was accepted again as a member on 30 June 1993 with retro-active effect as of 1 January 1993, but 18 March 1992 is still considered the date of ratification of Protocol No. 6 to the Convention.

As for the United Nations instruments, the Second Optional Protocol to the International Covenant on Civil and Political Rights Seeking Abolition of Death Penalty (1989) has been signed by the Slovak Republic in 1998. However, it has not yet been ratified.

Circumstances accompanying the abolition of the death penalty in 1990

The abolition of the death penalty in Czechoslovakia was not accompanied by any expert discussion. Generally it is understood as an exclusively political decision, the aim of which was the approximation of Czechoslovakia to a democratic Europe, namely to the Council of Europe. This has been confirmed by different theoreticians, for example Vlèek: "If the reason to abandon the death penalty has been an effort not to be left out of the European context, or Europeanism, then there is no need to seek any other grounds."

And the drafter of the Amendment to the Criminal Code held that "one of the arguments (in favour of the abolition of death penalty) was that the legislation to the contrary prevents the association of the country with some international organisations."

The Federal President Václav Havel was actively engaged in the abolition of death penalty and could be compared to François Mitterand and his influence upon the abolition of death penalty in France in 1981.

However, there was criticism mostly of the absence of arguments or supporting materials which could have been prepared by a commission of experts to be submitted to the Czechoslovak Federal Parliament and to the public. A variety of research-based materials and other relevant information concerning the death penalty could have formed a basis for further discussion and well-founded decisions. The debate in the Federal Parliament was marked by a lack of information, and by superficial and opportunist arguments. The entire debate concerning the drafted amendments of the Criminal Code, the Code of Criminal Procedure and of the Act on Punishment of Imprisonment lasted only two hours. And yet Czechoslovakia could have drawn on the expert experience from a similar group working for the same purposes for the Federal Parliament in 1968.

Deterrent effects of the death penalty in Slovakia

The criminal law policy to use the death penalty was justified mainly by the argument that the death penalty was able to protect society. The deterrent effect of the death penalty was often questioned; however, with the exception of the 1968 Expert Parliamentary Commission, no attempts to show proof of the preventive effects of death penalty were made.

The isolated conditions in which the death penalty was imposed and carried out in Slovakia, or in the former Czechoslovakia, made it all but impossible to apply standard methods for a study of the deterrent effects of the death penalty.

A comparison of the number of murder cases before and after the abolition of the death penalty

A comparison of the number of murder cases in the former Czechoslovakia before and after the abolition of death penalty as of 1 July 1990 would be significant in a stable social and political situation. The death penalty was abolished *de jure* on 1 July 1990. However, the abolition applied *de facto* since the beginning of January 1990, when far-reaching political and economic reforms were introduced in Czechoslovakia. That and other circumstances, such as President Havel's general pardon of January 1990 (when about thirty thousand inmates were released from prisons), or other factors of instability had a negative impact on the crime trends. The growth of violent and property crimes was alarming. In the first half of 1990 property crime in Slovakia increased by 116% when compared with the first half of 1989, and violent crime grew by 30.2% in the same period, that is, the number of robbery cases increased by 100.4%, murder cases by 65.6% and cases of rape by 42.3%. Out of the total number of known offenders prosecuted in Slovakia for crimes committed in the first half of 1990, 11.6 % were the former prisoners released from detention or prison as a result of President Havel's pardon in January 1990. Similar negative trends could be traced also in the Czech Republic. If standard methods of analysis of the deterrent effect of the death penalty were applied, a remarkable increase in murder cases and other forms of violent crime would be observed. But such a conclusion would be distorted and misleading, as the figures before and after the economic and social changes are comparable only on a relative basis.

A comparison of the number of murder cases in two similar jurisdictions, where the death penalty has been abolished in one jurisdiction, while it is imposed and executed in the other jurisdiction.

This method of analysis is not applicable, either. Czechoslovakia was committed to the activities of the former system of socialist countries until the end of 1989. With the exception of the German Democratic Republic, in which the death penalty was abolished in 1987, in the remaining countries of this bloc the death penalty was applicable to a smaller or greater extent. A comparison of Czechoslovakia with any other western European country would be impossible because of different political and economic situations.

A comparison of murder cases before and after an execution widely published through the mass media.

Execution of death sentences in cases of death penalty were never published in Czechoslovakia, or the notification was limited to a brief statement in the press. Therefore, it would be unreasonable to believe that existing communications could have any impact on the number of murders committed shortly after a brief notice in the newspapers, considering also that the number of murders committed per year in the whole of Czechoslovakia was relatively small, and a large number of murders were committed when the offenders were in a state of emotional distress.

Similarly inapplicable are the complicated economic methods of analysis of the deterrent effect of the death penalty (for example Grave's 1967 study[1] or Ehrlich's work of 1975[2]) used mainly in the United States. Apart from stability factors, these methods require also a balanced penal policy applied over several decades with criminal sanctions for the most serious crime. The existence of statistically significant data is also very important, nothing of which existed in Czechoslovakia with a varied history during forty years of development (second world war, the irrational 1950s, the 1968-69 period, the period of normalisation, 1989, etc.) and with a low number of murders and executions. If Ehrlich's approach were applied, the mere probability of executions for murder in Czechoslovakia before 1988 (a hundred persons convicted of murder, out of which two or three were executed annually), compared to the data from the United States, would indicate a result confirming the deterrent effect as exceeding the level presented in Ehrlich's study (according to which any execution results in the decrease of murder cases by seven or eight). This is not true in this country.

For Slovakia, or the former Czechoslovakia, the conclusion of an expert group led by Klein, a holder of the Nobel Prize for economics, dealing with the shocking results of the work by Ehrlich is applicable when claiming that "the deterrent effect of the death penalty is an open issue, and this fact is the most persuasive scientific outcome we have reached today". Knowing the situation in imposing and executing the death penalty in Slovakia, I would be very sceptical regarding any deterrent effect in the case of the ultimate punishment in my country.

The death penalty and public opinion in Slovakia

The first attempts to survey public attitudes towards the death penalty in Czechoslovakia occurred in 1947. The poll of May 1947 showed that 54% were against and 25% in favour of abolition of death penalty, and 21% not being able to give any answer. This survey was repeated in July 1947, after the death penalty was formally abolished for a short period of time in the Soviet Union, the results of which showed that 44 % were against and 36% in favour of abolition of death penalty with 20% not answering the question.

---

1. Grave in Gibbs, J., *Crime, Punishment and Deterrence*, Elsevier (New York: 1976), pp. 192-193.
2. Ehrlich I. in Hood, R., *Death Penalty. A Worldwide Perspective*, Clarendon Press (Oxford: 1989), p. 120.

So far the most extensive and most complex public survey on the death penalty was organised in June 1969 by the Research Institute of Criminology under the Office of General Prosecutor in co-operation with the Institute of Public Opinion of the Czechoslovak Academy of Sciences on the initiative of the Constitutional Committee of the Federal Parliament. Out of 1 263 respondents from all over Czechoslovakia, 33% were against and 51% in favour of the imposition of the death penalty, while 16% did not have any answer.

The draft of the amendment of the Criminal Code introducing abolition of the death penalty submitted to federal parliamentary debate in the first half of 1990 was another reason for a public poll. At that time, 49% were in favour of and 33% against the death penalty, with 18% of those not responding to the question. However, reliability and validity of these results was often discredited.

Currently, the attitude of the general public to the death penalty is significantly influenced by the following factors:

- a long tradition of imposition and execution of the death penalty;
- a low standard of legal awareness;
- an imperfect understanding of moral and ethical values and values of human life;
- a lack of objective information on the death penalty;
- a dramatic growth of crimes against life and health of others;
- an increase in organised crime and murders on request;
- the abolition of the death penalty as of 1 July 1990.

Taking into account the above facts and the response of the general public to the growing crime figures, one can assume that justification of the death penalty has been deeply rooted in the minds of the citizens (and also broad circles of lawyers). Therefore, in one of the fundamental issues of the current penal policy (criminal sanction for the most serious crimes being unquestionably one of them), the state cannot rely on the consent and credit of the citizens whose protection is its main concern. This is a logical consequence of ignoring the attitude of the general public to the death penalty. Therefore, we witness a considerable disparity between the penal policy of humanisation and liberalisation on the one hand and public opinion requiring stricter punishment for almost all crimes on the other. The increasing number of brutal crimes, that is offences against children and senior citizens, and also cases of murder as part of organised crime (out of 140 cases of murder committed in 1997, thirty cases were murders on request or liquidation murders which have not been solved) and their exposure through the mass media can result in increasing, unwanted pressure (especially now) upon the penal policy to use stricter forms of repression and consequently on the reduced imposition of the extraordinary sentences of imprisonment.

Controlling public opinion

A meaningful control of public opinion is one way of overcoming the unwanted gap between the state's policy on crime and public opinion. The degree of possible manipulation of the public's attitude to the death penalty was the aim of a minor sociological survey which I conducted at one secondary school in Slovakia at the end of 1990.

In the preparation of this experiment I presumed that public opinion can be remarkably controlled by very simple methods. I expected a shift in views on the death penalty and some other issues closely related to death penalty after the exposure of my respondents to a quantity of objective information concerning the death penalty.

At the start of the experiment, the students filled out a questionnaire without being advised on its purpose. The aim of the questionnaire was to give the students a chance to express their attitudes to the death penalty. Within the following month I addressed these topics with the students in the form of lectures and short discussions. The lectures tended to cover a wide range of issues by which I provided an objective view of the problems of the death penalty. After three weeks' lectures and discussions the students filled out the same questionnaire again. A comparison of the two questionnaires was meant to reveal a result of relevance to my hypothesis.

By a detailed analysis of the experiment, its weak points could be determined, too. However, the experiment confirmed – by a very simple method – how the state, through an appropriate choice of the means, could control the views of the public to such sensitive issues in its penal policy such as criminal sanctions in the most closely observed area of criminality. Quite naturally, there are other means of attaining a desirable compatibility. As regards the issues of the death penalty and other extraordinary sentencing, the focus should be on the provision of objective information regarding all aspects of penal policy upon which the citizens may build a rational evaluation of their views, and also on-going legal education from early childhood undertaken in the spirit of respect for human life.

Conclusion

The state's lack of interest in influencing the views of the general public regarding sanctions for the most serious of crimes is alarming. The gap between the official crime policy of the state in abolishing the death penalty and public opinion which expects the state to use the most extreme measures in its fight against crime (in the interest of the protection of life, health, freedom and property of the people) could become very broad and deep. The separation of the state from public opinion could be further magnified by the incredible growth of the most brutal crimes and the failure of government authorities to respond adequately. A possible consequence of this situation could be an uncontrollable and unmanageable public response to homicidal attacks against the weakest in society (such as children and the elderly).

Table 9.1 A survey of the number of executions and pardons (in the whole of Czechoslovakia)

Year	Executed	Pardoned
1970	–	–
1971	4	2
1972	2	-
1973	2	-
1974	3	-
1975	4	-
1976	2	-
1977	4	-
1978	3	-
1979	5	-
1980	2	-
1981	4	2
1982	1	-
1983	1	-
1984	5	-
1985	3	-
1986	2	-
1987	1	2
1988	2	-

10. A VAST PLACE OF EXECUTION – THE DEATH PENALTY IN RUSSIA

Anatoly Pristavkin, Chairman of the Presidential Pardons Commission of Russia

"We who are perishing in emigration, in untold torment for the whole of Russia that has become a gallows corner [*Lobnoye Mesto*]..." wrote the great Russian writer and Nobel Prize-winner Ivan Bunin, appalled by the endless death sentences carried out by the Bolsheviks after they came to power in 1917.

As anyone who has been in Russia knows, *Lobnoye Mesto* is a place in Moscow's Red Square where executions used to be carried out in former times.

But the "untold torment" for a Russia wallowing in cruelty and blood, which was experienced by our spiritual fathers, has not spared us either, for not that much has changed in Russia in the meantime. In any event, just as our whole nation believed it was necessary to kill more criminals, so we continue to believe this today. And the word "mercy" is little honoured among us. It is only our obligations *vis-à-vis* our European partners that are placing any sort of restraint upon our basic instincts. But for how long?

Three years have passed since Russia was admitted to the Council of Europe, in February 1996. As specified in the Parliamentary Assembly's Opinion No. 193, her admission was subject to her acceptance of certain commitments, including an undertaking to desist from carrying out death sentences immediately upon joining the Council of Europe. But at the Parliamentary Assembly's session in early 1997, it was stated that "the Parliamentary Assembly of the Council of Europe has received reliable information that, in the first half of 1996, fifty-three executions were carried out in Russia...", a fact constituting "a flagrant violation of her commitments and obligations". The Assembly went on to warn the Russian authorities that it would "take all necessary steps to ensure compliance with commitments entered into", including refusal to recognise the credentials of the Russian delegation.

I want to make it clear, and we have never concealed this, that the reports about the fifty-three executions (actually there were even rather more) reached the Council of Europe from our own Pardons Board. The authorities, as usual, said nothing. During the winter of 1996-97, a specially appointed group in the Russian Parliament, in which I myself took part, drew up a proposal for a moratorium on the application of the death penalty. Unfortunately, in March that year parliament rejected the proposal: there were only 75 votes in favour (one in every seven deputies) and 176 against – including the entire Communist Group, which has a parliamentary majority.

But, as I mentioned at the outset, the Bolsheviks' traditions, with their penchant for capital punishment, remain wholly intact. Even in the days of Lenin, who still appears on their banner, they boasted in the press of killing "exactly one thousand souls" in a single night in retaliation for the murder of just one leader, Uritskiy. All this occurred before the Stalinist abuses. Why then, one may ask, should our latter-day Bolsheviks now part with their favourite *Lobnoye Mesto*?

In general, the death penalty in Russia has its own long and painful history. The earliest written legal source, *Russian Truth*, says nothing about the death penalty at all. And Vladimir Monomakh's *Homily*, written soon after Russia's adoption of Christianity (tenth century), taught that it was wrong to kill either the just or the unjust.

The death penalty was enshrined in legislation only at the end of the fourteenth century, reaching its apogee during the reign of Ivan the Terrible (fifteenth century), when about four thousand people were executed. And under Peter the First, of whom Europe was so enamoured (seventeenth century), the death penalty could be imposed for as many as 123 different offences.

The earliest attempt to do away with capital punishment in Russia was made by Peter's daughter Elisabeth – for the first time in Europe, it is said – in the early eighteenth century. But it is the nineteenth century that may serve as some kind of yardstick for us; in the course of those one hundred years (a reputedly cruel period) the total number of executions was about 170. The death penalty was applicable to only three categories of offence: state crimes, military crimes, and anti-quarantine offences during epidemics. Neither for murder nor for robbery did our forefathers put people to death. For purposes of comparison, it may be noted that the Criminal Code that was rescinded only recently listed twenty-nine offences punishable by death. And it was not so long ago that women and children were still executed in our country, the latter from the age of 12 (Decree of 1935).

In 1962 alone, with the introduction of punitive laws against economic crimes (it will be recalled that these were timid attempts by individual entrepreneurs to bring about some change in the structure of the economy), about 3 000 people were shot. Eight killings a day! And this was going on in the very Khrushchev period which is looked back on approvingly as the thaw that set in after the rigours of the Stalinist winter.

From 1962 to 1990, a total of 21 000 people were executed in our country. It may be assumed that even this figure is on the low side; execution statistics have always been kept secret in Russia.

But it was also then, among the so-called "men of the sixties", that voices were first raised in protest against the acts of violence, the executions; and the most vociferous protester was Sakharov, followed by Sergei Kovalev, both of whom had personally experienced the full horrors of our penitentiary system.

Sakharov wrote:

> "The state in the person of its officials arrogates to itself the right to perform the most terrible and irreparable act – the taking of life. Such a state cannot expect any improvement in the country's moral climate. I reject the idea that the death penalty serves as any sort of significant deterrent for potential criminals. Indeed, I am convinced that the opposite is true, that savagery begets savagery."

In a popular television programme devoted to the problem of the death penalty, a large audience of young people were shown documentary footage of executions in America, after which there was a vote to see who was in favour of the death penalty; and it turned out that a majority of the audience were in favour. Then the question was put in a different way: who would be willing personally to carry out the sentence? And again a forest of hands rose up (over 80%). Soon those hands were to be firing guns at women and children in Chechnya. How all that ended we now know; it ended in those young lads being brought home in zinc coffins, and in their mothers being faced with an irreparable tragedy.

But my native Chechnya (where I spent my childhood) has so far been unable to restrain its own savagery either. The spectacle of public executions, conscientiously broadcast on every television channel, can arouse not only revulsion, which has been some people's reaction, but also a morbid interest followed by a wave of reciprocal cruelty – particularly, as we have seen, among the younger generation. And now we have someone writing to the newspapers and demanding a crackdown on economic criminals in Russia (we already know who they are), as is done in Chechnya. "I suggest taking them out into Red Square", he writes, "and letting the people stone them to death. After all, it would be a pity to waste bullets on them, as bullets are made with the people's money".

Believe me, there are plenty of such deluded souls. According to a survey conducted among the inhabitants of Moscow and St Petersburg (the two most enlightened major cities), 40% were in favour of public executions. For Russia as a whole the figure is even higher: 58%. People in the provinces, who mainly read the communist press, have an implicit faith in a "tough approach" which, by shooting enough recalcitrants, will finally restore an iron (Stalinist) order in the country. And if tomorrow such people are asked to elect a president, I fear they will vote for someone who will meet these requirements.

Unfortunately it is not only ordinary citizens that are calling for the shooting of criminals without investigation or trial, but also prominent and highly popular figures, including people in the arts. Recently one writer stated in an article that "the Americans wept for joy and danced when a terrorist was sentenced to death", which he described as "a healthy reaction by healthy people". Sadly, references to the authority of America and to its laws do much to strengthen the arguments of supporters of the death penalty.

The same writer expressed approval of cases where mobs have taken the law into their own hands that is, the lynching of criminals whom the courts in Russia have failed to sentence to death, calling this "a necessary defence against the impotence of the judiciary". Such calls for "self-defence", or in effect for lawlessness, are occasionally issued in the press by highly authoritative individuals.

And what can be said of the ordinary folk who inundate our Pardons Board with letters of protest when they learn that we have commuted the sentence of a prisoner on death row?

Let me say a few words about our Presidential Pardons Commission (the Pardons Board). It was born on the wave of enthusiasm and democratic hopes in early 1992, the first such body in Russian history. By some inexplicable miracle (our country is indeed a country of miracles), this mission of mercy was entrusted to the intelligentsia. In many ways the credit for this is due to the well-known human rights activist, Sergei Kovalev.

The Pardons Board was made up of well-known Russian personalities: poets, academics, priests, jurists, psychologists and the like, all on a public-service basis, although there is a great deal of work to be done. We meet once a week and in the course of a year consider five thousand cases, including about two hundred death sentences.

We are of course working in extreme conditions; sometimes we are misunderstood even by close friends and relatives, not to mention colleagues or acquaintances. We face pressure both from above and below – blackmail, telephone tapping, attempted bribery and phone calls threatening the lives of those dearest to us, all of which creates an atmosphere of nervousness and even mortal fear. Recently, for instance, one member of the Board, a professor at Moscow University, was twice attacked; thugs lay in wait for him at the entrance to his building and beat him savagely, cracking his skull.

Yet these people are all prominent figures in the cultural field, living – like most intellectuals – below the poverty line, with no money even for medicine (incidentally, the chairman of the Pardons Board, the current author, is in the same position). And here is this tiny "guard" resisting almost single-handed the powerful movement of those who support the death penalty.

It is possible that the attempts to neutralise or eliminate us will include calumny, the forgery of compromising materials and even deliberate provocations. But we have no other defence than our good name.

Although the number of executions carried out in Russia between 1995 and 1996 was enormous (139), I can assure you it would have been three times higher but for the desperate efforts of my friends to save each life. We have looked to the future and tried to divert our country from the disastrous course along which we have been impelled by short-sighted government officials. Recently they practically succeeded in eliminating the Pardons Board, and had almost a hundred condemned prisoners shot. Now, thank God, the granting of pardons has been restored. And no death sentence has been carried out for more than a year.

It must be said that particular zeal in seeking to maintain and even increase the number of executions has always been displayed by two all-powerful monsters: Russia's Public Prosecutor's Office and its Ministry of the Interior. Their argument is simple: crime is increasing, and abolition of the death penalty will cause it to increase even further.

There is another argument too, at first sight a fairly convincing one: the public horror generated by the phenomenon of organised crime. But among the hundreds of people executed (or pardoned) while we have been at work, not one case of a mafioso, hired killer or terrorist has yet come before our Board.

Mafia-type structures and the mingling of government and militia circles with organised crime have taken on truly nationwide dimensions.

Underworld bosses are becoming members of parliament, district governors and the like, and there is not the slightest prospect of their being brought to justice.

Whom are we executing, then? The people the state executes are from the lowest, most defenceless layer of society, besotted with vodka and reduced to a bestial condition; they usually commit their run-of-the-mill crimes when drunk; 80% or more of the cases that come before us involve offences committed in a state of drunkenness.

Naturally, these wretches are unable to defend themselves or hire expensive lawyers. And, of course, some of them confess under the influence of "non-standard investigative methods", such as torture. Recently the newspapers carried a story about how two militiamen extorted a murder confession out of an innocent man by means of subtle taunting and eventually killed him by forcing three Cola bottles up his rear passage. And neither we nor anyone else can be sure that our very own Ministry of the Interior will not cover up their crime and thus enable them, like many of their comrades, to escape trial.

But even when such people do end up in the dock (one in ten, it is said), there are special prisons for them, where the conditions are perfectly humane.

The statistics, too, suggest that crime in the very ranks of the militia has reached incredible proportions, and those questioned in a recent survey (60% to 80% of them were victims) said they never asked the militia for help, as they feared the militia most of all – far more, indeed, than gangsters. But it often turns out that the two groups are one and the same anyway.

Now we have a scandal erupting in the Kuzbass, where the militia has helped a gang leader to become mayor. The same sort of thing is going on in Zlatoust, in the Urals, and in other regions. "General criminalisation" – that is the reality of Russia, from members of parliament to city mayors. As the Minister of the Interior reported recently, about fifty deputies at various levels are former convicts, all with a long criminal record. It is difficult to imagine this, but 15% of the entire adult population of Russia has spent time in camps and prisons.

Prominent jurists claim that miscarriages of justice are now running at a rate of 10% to 15% or more even among persons condemned to death. And at the same time a series of highly sensational murder cases in recent years have yet to be cleared up. A legitimate question arises: is one reason why the death penalty is necessary is that it helps to conceal our authorities' inability to control the rising crime wave? A number of innocent people have already confessed to the murder of Father Menya (a celebrated preacher of goodness and peace who had a wide following among simple folk); if the authorities manage to execute any of them, the problem of finding the real criminals would vanish and the public would sleep peacefully.

Our rulers have yet another, seemingly very serious argument – the economic argument, which they use to scare both the impoverished masses and the élite. If, they say, we now bow to the wishes of the Council of Europe and pardon six or seven hundred people all at once (that is how many are at present awaiting the death sentence), it will cost billions and billions of roubles to build new camps and prisons as well as to keep the prisoners themselves. This is not such a feeble argument in view of the exiguity of our budget.

But here, too, they are lying. The inmates of our camps and prisons currently total 1.2 million, almost ten times more per head of population than in any civilised country; and the addition of another 500 or so (representing no more than 0.05%) cannot harm the budget.

The fact that 300 000 of them, or one in four, are languishing in pre-trial detention (in so-called Sizos or isolation cells), where they wait for years to be put on trial, is another matter – and most of them are young people.

We recently had referred to us the case of someone who spent six years in pre-trial detention. And more than half of such people, if indeed they are ever brought to trial, are then released for lack of evidence.

People die in the cells from overcrowding and from illness (more often than not tuberculosis); they take turns sleeping; they go blind, deaf and even mad before ever coming to trial. In the famous Butyrsk prison in Moscow about 300 non-convicted people die every year.

And these are losses that our rulers, for some reason, leave out of the account. Yet in essence they are also executions, carried out without trial and recorded by no one. And no one will ever be held responsible for them.

So, the usual stereotypes about the penitentiary system as a repressive, gulag-style system that humiliates and debases its inmates still hold sway in our correctional institutions.

What, then, can be said about the camps set up for death-row prisoners whom we have pardoned? These camps are run along the same gulag lines in the depths of the taiga, where the most elementary medical care is lacking, not to mention psychological or other kinds of help (the inmates being denied the right to take exercise, meet people or receive information from outside in the form of newspapers or mail).

The Pardons Board was rather proud of itself when it succeeded a few years ago in pushing through parliament a law on life imprisonment as an alternative to the death penalty. But surely such a painful existence is also a kind of death sentence, albeit spread out in time. And now rumours are reaching us of suicides in these camps; we are getting letters from despairing prisoners who beg us to rescind their pardon and execute them so as to put them out of their misery.

Since August 1996, even though there is no law banning the death penalty in Russia, not a single prisoner has been shot in our country. Upon our initiative, which was supported by the President, there is a tacit moratorium as a result of which we no longer deal with capital cases. But, of course, such a situation cannot last long; if there were change of government tomorrow, the firing squads would set to work again with renewed energy, to the general approval of the people, as is already happening in Chechnya.

Indeed, calls for the shooting to begin again continue to flood the newspapers. When preparing this article, I looked through some newspapers and magazines published in the past few months and found about ten or so demands for the resumption of executions.

And the ink of our signature to Protocol No. 6 on the prohibition of the death penalty was barely dry when our Prosecutor General, Skuratov, again wrote to the President arguing that "our country is not yet ready for the abolition of the death penalty" and recommending that "the application and execution of the death penalty be set in order". "Order", according to Skuratov, is when people are shot. And these demands are dangerous, in my view, because they come not from some casual passer-by wishing to enjoy bloody spectacles in Red Square, but from the first law officer in the land, who is in a position to exert genuine influence on such decisions. And he has powerful allies who support him both in the government and in parliament.

And now a few words about parliament, where a proposal for a moratorium on the carrying out of the death penalty that was tabled by deputy Borshchev in summer 1998 has twice been rejected. The elected representatives of our people are not prepared to approve it ever. I am talking about a moratorium on executions, not about a ban on the death penalty as such, as a law banning the death penalty does not even exist in draft form; nor is there any prospect of one.

I have touched upon just some of the problems that are causing us concern at present.

We must not delude ourselves, the campaign to do away with the death penalty in Russia will be fierce, and its outcome is as yet unpredictable. As law professor Valeriy Savitskiy put it when addressing the Russian Parliament, in order to solve this problem we must find a way of combining legal and ethical standards. I agree with him – although in Russia there have always been problems with ethics. I agree, too, with his forthright assertion that either we will remain decent people in a decent society or we are simply liars and unfit to be in the European community.

11. Abolishing the death penalty in Ukraine – difficulties real or imagined?

Serhiy Holovatiy, President of the Ukrainian Legal Foundation, member of parliament, Ukraine

---

Introduction

Summer 1991. During the Mikhail Gorbachev era, glasnost and perestroika facilitated the turning point in the history of many of nations in the communist world and finally opened the door to freedom, independence, and the path toward democracy.

August 1991 was a defining month in the history of Ukraine. It was among the first Soviet republics to declare independence following the collapse of the Moscow communist regime in Ukraine. On 1 December 1991, a nationwide referendum ultimately confirmed Ukraine's status as an independent state and for the first time in their history, Ukrainians elected their own President as of the head of state. At this time I was a people's deputy of Ukraine, elected to the Verkhovna Rada, Ukraine's Parliament, on a pro-democracy, anti-communist platform in March 1990.

The late 1980s and early 1990s were the formative years of my political career. Ironically, it was during this period that I became aware of the complexity and bitterness regarding the issue of the death penalty. It was at this time that I was directly confronted by this problem, both as a human being and as a politician.

In the autumn of 1991, immediately following Ukraine's declaration of independence, the relatives of a young man sentenced to death asked me for my help as a people's deputy. The young man had been wrongly accused and charged with the murder of the son of one of the leaders of Soviet Ukraine. The criminal case had been adjudicated by the Supreme Court of the Ukrainian SSR in the first instance prior to Ukraine's declaration of independence and the death sentence imposed on the eve of independence. At that time, verdicts by the Ukrainian court could be appealed to the USSR Supreme Court. As a result of Ukraine's declaration of independence and national sovereignty on 24 August 1991, the USSR Supreme Court ceased to have jurisdiction on the territory of Ukraine. Therefore, the sentenced person was deprived of his right to appeal. He applied to the State Commission of Pardons, which until 1 December 1991, was subordinate to the presidium of the Verkhovna Rada of the Ukrainian SSR. The commission ordered a pardon and it seemed as though the life of the young man was saved.

On 1 December 1991, the nation elected the President of Ukraine. The father of the murder victim continued to occupy one of the leading posts in the state. A new Commission of Pardons was established under the President, which reviewed the case of the sentenced person and revoked the previous decision to pardon him without giving any reasons. His relatives were in a panic; nobody could understand what had happened.

They turned to me for help. I was shown a letter passed on to them from their condemned son in which he explained to his father, mother and wife that he was not involved in the murder. He maintained that his confession was obtained under duress and intimidation in prison; he was told that if he did not confess, his parents, wife and two children would be killed, and to protect the lives of his parents and children, he admitted to committing the crime.

The next day, I approached the newly-appointed first Prosecutor General of an independent Ukraine. I tried to convince him that arbitrariness and injustice had taken place. He appeased me, saying: "Don't worry, we'll remedy the situation. Sentenced persons are not executed that quickly. Not earlier than in half a year... There is time." One or two days after the Commission of Pardons made its decision and I had met with the Prosecutor General, he informed me that the young man had been summarily executed in Kyiv.

The lightning speed with which events unfolded, the use of state law enforcement institutions to satiate the indisputable personal interest on the part of top state officials, the summary execution of a human being whose actual guilt was not proved, the anguish of the young man's parents and relatives had a profound impact on my views towards the death penalty. I realised that the national independence for which I had struggled would not automatically protect the rights of the state's citizens. I did not simply want to live in an independent Ukraine. I wanted a state where human freedoms are securely grounded in the rule of law and where citizens have the right to life and due process before the law, protected from the exercise of arbitrary power by the state. I also realised that the struggle for these values in Ukraine would be a difficult one, as the state held, and continues to hold, monopoly control over the exercise of these rights.

An attempt to solve the problem on both an institutional and a legislative level

On 26 September 1995, the Parliamentary Assembly of the Council of Europe (PACE) recommended in Opinion No. 190 that the Committee of Ministers of the Council of Europe admit Ukraine to the Council of Europe. In this connection, Ukraine undertook a series of obligations, including the obligation to impose a moratorium on executions from the day of accession, 9 November 1995, and to ratify Protocol No. 6 to the European Convention on Human Rights within three years.

On 27 September 1995, while in Strasbourg, as a member of the Ukrainian parliamentary delegation to the historic debate concerning Ukraine's accession at the PACE, I was informed that I had been appointed Minister for Justice of Ukraine in accordance with a decree issued by the President of Ukraine.

The coincidental occurrence of these two events – one in the political life of my country and the other in my political career – was for me much more than merely symbolic. I immediately realised that henceforth I carried the political responsibility for implementing a state legal policy in accordance with Opinion No. 190. My objective was very clear: I had to ensure that the activities of the President and the cabinet of ministers were conducted in a manner consistent with Ukraine's international commitments and to integrate the norms and standards of the Council of Europe into Ukraine's domestic legal system. Of paramount importance was the protection of human rights and the imposition of a moratorium on the application of the death penalty.

The support promised by the President of Ukraine with respect to the implementation of these objectives, however, turned out to be short-lived. In October 1995, the President appointed a new Prosecutor General, an old-style classical representative of the Soviet system of power and Soviet morality. During his first press conference on 27 October 1995, the newly-appointed Prosecutor General criticised the policy of the Council of Europe regarding the death penalty, calling it a "dictate" to Ukraine and stated that the idea of abolishing the death penalty in Ukraine is unacceptable, notwithstanding that Ukraine voluntarily took upon itself to perform this obligation. These statements were made two weeks before Ukraine's official accession to the Council of Europe. As Minister for Justice I was forced to make an official statement refuting the statements by the Prosecutor General, and which I characterised as a "stab in the back of Ukraine" on the eve of its accession into the Council of Europe.

These two contradictory official statements regarding the death penalty by two of the top legal officials in the state, which were in direct contradiction to each other, gave rise to a storm of journalistic publications concerning the death penalty in Ukraine. Most of these supported the statement made by the Prosecutor General.

The Prosecutor General's public opposition to the idea of abolishing the death penalty in Ukraine could not have taken place without the consent of the President. Thus, while not yet even a member of the Council of Europe, Ukraine's leaders demonstrated their reluctance to implement Ukraine's commitments regarding the abolition of the death penalty at the institutional level. Thus, the introduction of a single state legal policy regarding this issue was threatened from the very start. This threat was further methodically manifested by various bodies of state power either through the open denial of the need to abolish the death penalty, or sometimes through the latent sabotage of measures designed to promote the abolitionist policy.

As the Ministry of Justice found itself increasingly isolated within the system of bodies of state power regarding the issue of the death penalty, we began to look for other ways to institutionally secure our policy. These resulted in the following measures.

- Pursuant to the proposal of the Ministry of Justice, on 11 March 1998 the President of Ukraine established a State Inter-Agency Commission on the Implementation of the Norms and Standards of the Council of Europe into Ukrainian Legislation (the State Commission). Chaired by the Minister for Justice, the commission's mandate was to co-ordinate the activities of the cabinet of ministers, parliament, the Supreme Court, the office of the Prosecutor General and the presidential administration regarding the implementation of Opinion No. 190. The moratorium on the death penalty was a priority issue for the commission. On 18 June 1996, the State Commission approved the Justice Minister's proposal regarding the establishment of a special commission to facilitate the abolition of the death penalty.

- Accordingly, on 21 August 1996, the President of Ukraine established the Commission on Elaborating Issues Related to Abolishing the Death Penalty. This commission was headed by the President's Legal Policy Adviser, a professor and a prominent Ukrainian criminal law scholar, who had never hidden his abolitionist views. The commission was charged with the task of preparing proposals for the President on abolishing the death penalty, suspending executions and introducing an alternative form of punishment in Ukraine, including life imprisonment.

- On the Justice Minister's initiative, on 20 March 1997 the State Commission, the Commission on Elaborating Issues Related to Abolishing the Death Penalty and members of the Ukrainian national parliamentary delegation to the PACE held a joint meeting. The meeting resulted in a decision to accelerate ratification of the European Convention on Human Rights, to sign Protocol No. 6 and to declassify information regarding capital punishment sentences in Ukraine.

In addition to the foregoing institutional and organisational initiatives, the Ministry of Justice also developed a number of legislative proposals regarding the abolition of the death penalty in Ukraine, including:

- on 4 April 1996, a law drafted by the Ministry of Justice on amending the Criminal Code to substitute the death penalty with an alternative punishment of life imprisonment was submitted to the Verkhovna Rada of Ukraine for the first time (although the draft was subsequently sent back to the Ministry of Justice with no reasons given for the return);

- on 29 January 1997, the Ministry of Justice submitted a draft law on amending the Criminal Code to the cabinet of ministers, in which it proposed to substitute the death penalty with life imprisonment and to introduce a moratorium on executions. The Minister of Internal Affairs, the Chief of the Security Service, the President of the Supreme Court, the Minister for Foreign Affairs, and the Prosecutor General of Ukraine all approved the draft. On 19 April, however, the draft was defeated by the Verkhovna Rada due to "the absence of financial calculations" on the cost of introducing life imprisonment as an alternative form of punishment;

- on 12 June 1997, the cabinet of ministers submitted for consideration to the Verkhovna Rada a draft of the new Criminal Code, which did not contain the death penalty. The new code had been drafted by a working group headed by the Minister for Justice;

- on 26 June 1997, the cabinet of ministers submitted to the Verkhovna Rada for consideration a draft law on changes to the Criminal Code with supplementary financial calculations of expenditures with respect to introducing life imprisonment as an alternative form of punishment to the death penalty.

To date, neither of the last two draft laws have been considered in parliament.

Opposition from Ukranian society

Since Ukraine became a member of the Council of Europe, the death penalty has become the subject of intensive discussion in society, especially in the mass media. Over the last two years, nearly 400 analytical articles, interviews, reports and notes devoted to the question of abolition of the death penalty have been published in Ukraine's leading newspapers alone.

The items vary considerably in terms of their emotional, statistical and analytical content. The frequency of their publication is not evenly paced. As a rule, every periodic wave of publications is either connected with discussion of the "Ukrainian issue" at a session of the PACE, a visit by a delegation from the Council of Europe to Ukraine, in relation to the holding of a seminar devoted to this subject, or another heinous act of murder by a killer who arouses the rage of the entire nation.

Thus, the arrest of a mass murderer named Onupriyenko (he is blamed for fifty-two killings) in the spring of 1997, produced an explosive reaction in the press. The arrest, unfortunately, did not take place in time to save the life of an innocent 27-year-old man, wrongly convicted and executed for Onupriyenko's crimes. It was argued by some (including this author) that the absence of judicial safeguards and sufficient due process to protect the rights of the accused in Ukraine in capital cases was as good a reason as any to stay the application of the death penalty. Nevertheless, society's opinion regarding this issue remains steadfastly pro-death penalty. People doubt the state's ability "to build strong enough prisons that will guarantee that sadists and rapists will never break free from them".[1] The population's view is driven by a fear of an unprotected society in the uncertain economic environment wrought by the lack of reform in Ukraine, coupled with the legacy of a "life is cheap" ideology inherited from Soviet times.

These sentiments are reflected in the press. "Abolishing the death penalty in our society is criminal madness! This is the opinion of those who uncover crimes and catch killers." This headline, which in essence conveys the substance of the publication in the *Den* newspaper, emphasises the fact that "every three years, starting from 1992, the death rate of people murdered at the hands of killers in Ukraine is as high as Soviet army casualties during the war in Afghanistan. Every day – twelve killings".[2]

This type of reminder in many publications continually strengthens society's attitude to the principle of "an eye for an eye, a tooth for a tooth."

Society's attitude towards the death penalty has become the subject of continual study by various sociological services that research public opinion. For example, the following data was provided in the *Uriadovyi Kurier* newspaper (17 September 1996) regarding a 1996 study conducted by the Institute of Sociology of the National Academy of Sciences of Ukraine, the Democratic Initiatives Centre and the Socis-Gallup service:

---

1. The *Tyzhden* newspaper, 27 February 1997.
2. The *Den* newspaper, 5 April 1998.

Table 11.1: Ukranian society's attitude towards the death penalty

Answers (in percentage)	1994	1995	1996
Abolish immediately	5	4	6
Make gradual progress toward abolition	12	12	12
Leave application according to current proportions	32	36	40
Expand its application	35	33	23
Difficult to answer	16	15	18

Therefore, the number of those supporting the immediate abolition of the death penalty was not great, although the percentage of those in favour of expanding the application of the death penalty was significantly lower. Women leaned toward leaving everything the way it is now. Among the men, there were more who advocated making progress toward abolishing the death penalty. Those with higher education and young people expressed more humane sentiments. The study revealed positive correlations between support for the abolition of the death penalty and the level of support for market reforms and democracy, and negative correlations, in terms of an authoritarian outlook. Of special interest for the study was the stance of representatives from those social groups which directly influence societal development, specifically, members of parliament and journalists. Their responses were much more tolerant than those expressed by society as a whole; journalists and members of parliament felt that it was time to gradually move toward abolishing the death penalty.

As other sociological studies have shown, the citizens of Ukraine are firm in their public belief concerning the need to maintain the death penalty. According to data from one study,[1] at the beginning of 1997, 62% of 1 050 respondents spoke in favour of more intensively applying the death penalty; 81% of those polled were convinced about its effect as a deterrent on persons prone to commit crimes; 80% viewed it as being necessary retribution for the commission of a crime. Thus, the overwhelming majority of respondents believed that the threat of severe punishment will restrain a person from committing a crime.

---

1. The *Den* newspaper, 12 February 1997.

This negative attitude toward abolition of the death penalty is also confirmed by the results of a public opinion poll that was conducted by the Socis-Gallup service in April 1997. Out of 1 200 of those polled 43% believed that the death penalty should not be abolished, 37% thought that it should be utilised only in exceptional instances, 15% believed that it should be completely abolished, and 5% found this question difficult to answer. However, the data from this study indicated a slight weakening of society's harsh position on the death penalty and a tendency towards an acceptance of the abolition of the death penalty since the number of those who supported the idea of abolishing the death penalty had increased in comparison with a similar poll conducted in January 1995 and 1996. According to respondents, the main reason why the death penalty should be preserved as a punishment is that Ukraine is still not ready to abolish the death penalty (44%). Every third respondent believes that the death penalty restricts the increase of crime in the country and every fifth one believes that "by executing the criminal, society can protect itself from the repeated offence".[1] Nevertheless, this notion of the importance of punishment in the battle against crime is indicative of Ukrainian society's underdeveloped legal culture and the prevalence of authoritarian views shaped during Soviet times. It also reflects the fear and insecurity of a society in the process of transition to a democracy and a market economy.

However, the extent and intensity of opposition to the abolition of the death penalty is not uniform throughout the country. Among residents in western Ukraine (which was under the oppression of communism only since 1939) public opinion seems to be evenly divided over whether to completely abolish the death penalty. On the one hand, out of 500 residents polled in Halychyna, 50.4% believe that the "death penalty should be preserved even if Ukraine loses the support of European countries". However, 44.4% adhere to another view: "Ukraine should enter European structures without any hindrances even if the death penalty has to be abolished". The rest of those polled had no views on the subject.

Therefore, as different polls indicate, public opinion in Ukraine does not, at present, view Ukraine's obligations before the Council of Europe as a persuasive argument in favour of abolishing the death penalty.

True, a seminar specifically designed for journalists entitled Cancelling the Death Penalty, held by the Council of Europe in conjunction with the Ministry of Justice and the Ukrainian Legal Foundation in the spring of 1997, influenced to a degree the content and character of further publications. Journalists are beginning to make attempts to raise public awareness of the

---

1. The *Den* newspaper, 25 May 1997.

fact that execution *per se* may be construed as a crime and that the death penalty is not an indigenous Ukrainian phenomenon; it was introduced into Ukrainian society in the sixteenth century by Russian imperial legislation.

The state's inactivity

The principal problem regarding this issue is the total lack of leadership on the part of the President and other key state authorities. Indeed, journalists themselves are starting to widely assert that the state should take a role in forming public opinion rather than following its lead. The state, after all, has the capacity to acquire and disseminate to the public information and studies which prove that the death penalty is an illusory and ineffective solution to controlling the problem of violent crime. Indeed, the majority of countries have abolished the death penalty despite powerful public opposition. "Can public opinion assume obligations which are placed on politicians and persons who make specific decisions?" ask journalists and reply at the same time: "Referring to public opinion in this situation is a way of finding a good excuse for inactivity and the desire to shift responsibility onto others' shoulders."

Unfortunately, the executions in Ukraine continue unabated and with seemingly renewed vigour. From the time of its admission into the Council of Europe, Ukraine has firmly maintained its lead position with regard to implementing death sentences. Top officials have confirmed the state's position in the following terms: "Principally, we are in favour of abolishing the death penalty." It is difficult to understand what the word "principally" means. If it means "in principle" then decisive moves to abolish the death penalty could have been made immediately. This, however, has not happened. Instead, for more than three years, Ukraine has been playing games with its commitments to the Council of Europe. This is happening at both the executive and the legislative levels with each level of power castigating the other for non-performance of Ukraine's commitments. The President either brings charges against the Verkhovna Rada for its stubborn denial of efforts to remove articles related to the death penalty from the Criminal Code, its refusal to adopt the new Criminal Code, its initial reluctance to ratify Protocol No. 6, and so on. The President, for his part, flatly refuses to sign the decree prepared by the Ministry of Justice imposing a moratorium on the execution of death sentences which was submitted to him in February 1997 (this is exclusively the President's prerogative). The President has also evaded meeting the requirements of the Parliamentary Assembly of the Council of Europe to send an official statement on introducing the moratorium in Ukraine and has delegated this responsibility to the Minister for Foreign Affairs. In this way, the President has attempted to distance himself from responsibility for the consequences of government assurances to the Council of Europe that the death penalty is not being applied in Ukraine, when in fact it is.

Further, no effort has been made to change the policies concerning the application of the death penalty in relevant ministries and other central agencies subordinate to the President. In particular, Ukraine is the only country in Europe which has not eliminated the regime of secrecy with regard to the execution of death penalties, a matter which can be rectified by a presidential decree.

The principal opponents in government to abolishing the death penalty have been heads of the so-called "power institutions": the Ministry of Internal Affairs, the State Security Service and the Prosecutor General's Office. Utilising statistical data on the crime rate as a major argument in favour of their anti-abolitionist stance, they perpetuate the myth that the death penalty needs to be applied to restrain crime. They cite data such as: in 1991, 2 902 killings were registered, in 1992 – 3 679, in 1993 – 4 008, in 1994 – 4 571, in 1995 – 4 783, and in 1996 – 4 896.

They follow the lead of the President. In September 1996, addressing a congress of judges, President Kuchma said that during a period of unstable social and political transition, violent crime is steadily rising, which accentuates the need to study further the issue of whether the death penalty should or should not be abolished. During a meeting with an official delegation from the Council of Europe in Ukraine in November 1996, the chairman of the Verkhovna Rada emphasised that "the country's crime rate does not allow for cancelling the death penalty".

Unfortunately, this same view was also voiced by leaders of one of the largest lawyers' organisations in Ukraine. The head of the Union of Lawyers' of Ukraine, who also currently heads the High Council of Justice has stated that: "An immediate abolition of the death penalty has not been prepared and can, in today's circumstances, even lead to an increase in the number of victims suffering from the most dangerous crimes."[1]

The Council of Europe is losing ground in its continuous efforts to restrain Ukraine from applying the death penalty. Indeed, Ukrainian officials have been reduced to lying and disgracing themselves with respect to official data concerning the number of executions performed. In August 1997, the Deputy Minister for Justice officially stated that in the first six months of 1997, thirteen persons were executed and seventy-three persons were sentenced to death in Ukraine. The negative resonance from this information

---

1. The *Holos Ukrainy* newspaper, 2 July 1997.

during the September session of the Parliamentary Assembly of the Council of Europe caused top Ukrainian leaders to try to muddy the waters, which ultimately resulted in an open lie. In October 1997, Minister for Justice S. Stanik disavowed the official statement made by her deputy, qualifying it as a "result of a statistical error" and stated that acts of execution have not been committed in Ukraine since January 1997. The minister repeated this same statement during the Second Summit of Heads of State and Government of the Council of Europe in Strasbourg (10-11 October), although the President of Ukraine at the summit himself announced that the last act of execution was committed in Ukraine on 11 March 1997. Other officials from the presidential administration, government and other Ukrainian bodies of power provided fairly conflicting data on acts of execution including those which Minister Stanik personally handed the President of the Parliamentary Assembly Leni Fischer during the January 1998 session of the Parliamentary Assembly, which claimed that only nine persons were executed in the course of the entire year of 1997.

Since Ukraine has been a member of the Council of Europe, none of the state leaders has ever demonstrated their political will, courage or determination to keep the promise which was made before Ukraine's admission, that is to fulfil all requirements put forward to Ukraine in connection with its membership of the Council of Europe. Instead, the parliament, two years before elections (which took place in March 1998), and the President, in the run-up to the presidential election in October 1999, have repeatedly demonstrated political cowardice by abdicating any leadership on this issue.

The judiciary seems to be taking its cue from the conduct of the other branches of power as well. It seems as though this disgraceful situation could have been resolved by the Constitutional Court of Ukraine. In March 1997, forty-six national deputies appealed to the Constitutional Court, challenging the constitutionality of Article 24 of the Criminal Code of Ukraine, the death penalty provision, pursuant to Article 3 (the right to life) and Article 28 (the right to respect of dignity) of the Constitution of Ukraine. The President of Ukraine supported the idea of the possibility of resolving the issue of abolishing the death penalty in Ukraine through the authority of the Constitutional Court. But on 4 December 1997, the Constitutional Court declined to hear the application. The circle was complete.

Conclusions

Instead of making formal conclusions, I would like to cite statements made by three compatriots, colleagues from the legal profession: a judge, and two military instructors at educational establishments in the internal affairs administration.

Mykola Luhovyi, a judge:

"When you receive the notice about the execution of 'your' death penalty verdict, your soul moans as if it wants to free itself from an incredible sin but cannot do so..." (The *Kiyevskiye Vedomosti* newspaper, 22 April 1994).

Olha Shevchenko, militia lieutenant colonel:

"The majority of the population has over almost eighty years of existing in a totalitarian state managed to become accustomed to the idea that it has always lived with the death penalty and cannot live without it. But actually, if we are to recall history, the idea of the death penalty never belonged to the Ukrainian people. This type of punishment has never been characteristic of Ukraine. ... In the history of not only our nation but practically all other nations of the world, this exceptional form of punishment manifested itself as the result of political strife in society. During the Soviet era, the Ukrainian state, in its battle against crime, demonstrated complete feebleness and actual weakness and tried to compensate for this by applying the death penalty to its own citizens... We have already lived in fear of the death penalty. Now, let's try to live without it!" (The *Iurydychnyi Visnyk Ukrainy* newspaper, 1-7 May 1997).

Georghiy Radov, President of the Kyiv Institute of Internal Affairs, Major General:

"It is society that is largely to blame for the crimes committed in it, for it is the environment which fills the human will with evil and criminal tendencies, and is the cause of crimes rather than an individual evil will. Crime is a symptom of the illness of society itself... The punishments applied by the state indicate society's level of moral development. The low level of morality creates a cruel system of punishment..."

"Preserving the death penalty in Ukraine's system of criminal punishments is contradictory to the strategic course pursued by its institutes in domestic and foreign policy and the commitment assumed before the international community which cannot but leave its imprint on the prestige of our state." (The *Den* newspaper, 12 February 1997).

Despite the current atmosphere in Ukraine concerning the death penalty, these opinions, shared by many others, may provide the foundation for optimism that through leadership, public awareness initiatives and the courage of the legal profession to speak out against capital punishment, Ukraine may still enter the twenty-first century without the death penalty.

Conclusion

Sergei Kovalev, Russian parliamentarian, received the Council of Europe Human Rights Prize in 1995

The debate over the abolition of the death penalty has been going on for many years and, I fear, is likely to continue for many more to come. Supporters and opponents of the death penalty have, it would seem, already said all there is to say on the subject. Had this collection included contributions from both sides of the debate, I might well have been tempted to set out the abolitionist argument yet again. As it happens, however, the authors of this publication are of one mind, so my energies would probably be better employed trying to understand the very nature of the debate and the psychological and cultural barriers that prevent many people from adopting our point of view.

Possibly there are flaws in our line of reasoning. For instance, I would like to pose a question: we abolitionists are forever trying to prove to people that the abolition of the death penalty does not lead to an increase in crime. Are we saying that were this fact not borne out by statistics, we would have no scruples about siding with those who believe that the death penalty ought to be maintained? It is my belief (and hope!) that the majority of abolitionists would still call for it to be abolished. What makes us think, then, that an argument which we ourselves regard as essentially secondary, albeit statistically accurate, is going to cut any ice with our opponents?

The same logic applies to the dispute over the economic expediency – or inexpediency – of replacing the death penalty with life imprisonment.

Another argument often invoked by abolitionists is the moral dilemma experienced by the individuals whose job it is to carry out death sentences. I, for one, suspect that the professional executioner who suffers torments of remorse is a fairly rare phenomenon. But even supposing we accepted the truth of this argument, surely it would not be too difficult, with modern technology, to automate the execution process, thereby removing any sense of personal responsibility? Incidentally, that grisly invention that greeted mankind at the dawn of the modern age, the guillotine, was devised as a "painless" means of punishment, which had the added advantage of enabling at least part of the executioner's job to be performed by a machine. Of course, the guillotine was only the first step in this direction. Today in some parts of the world, for example, in certain states of the USA, moves are already under way to have executions performed with the aid of computers. If we truly believed this moral argument to be fundamental, however, why do we bother to fight against the death penalty *per se*, instead of just being content with improving the technology?

One might say in reply that, for the abolitionist, all these considerations are indeed merely secondary, but for those who do not share our point of view, they are often decisive.

Frankly I doubt that. I do not believe that we abolitionists, as a whole, are any more compassionate or unselfish than our opponents. Which of us has not clenched our fists and felt our blood rise on hearing of some particularly brutal crime? Which of us has not conjured up in our mind's eye the faces of those responsible? The desire for vengeance is a perfectly natural human reaction. This, incidentally, is where the oft-cited (including in this publication) analogy between the death penalty and such antiquated institutions as torture or slavery ends. For it is difficult to see how, even in days gone by, any normal person who professed a strong emotional attachment to torture or who claimed the right to own another human being could be acting from anything other than selfish (in the broad sense of the term) motives. Whereas supporters of the death penalty are no more selfish than we are. Nor are they any more inclined to sadism. Their support for the death penalty stems from a natural human revulsion at the crimes in question, pity for the victims, anger and indignation.

It is simply that we abolitionists are willing to suppress these emotions, allowing ourselves to be governed instead by – what? Religious beliefs?

The fact is that there are probably just as many religious believers among supporters of capital punishment as there are atheists among its opponents. Not all world religions, moreover, deny categorically the right to kill. And even among those religious leaders whose faith does absolutely and unequivocally rule out capital punishment, there are still some individuals who would argue that these interdictions are "relative". Legend has it that a thousand years ago, Prince Vladimir of Kiev, having been converted to Christianity, proposed abolishing the death penalty in Rus and that it was the priests, of all people, who talked him out of it, saying that the teachings of Christ should not be taken too literally.

In 1990 and 1991, as a member of the Praesidium of the Supreme Soviet of the RSFSR, I was sometimes called upon to hear appeals for clemency. Whenever we were asked to rule on appeals from persons facing the death penalty, I, in keeping with my beliefs, invariably voted for them to be granted. And, equally invariably, another member of the Praesidium, an Orthodox priest, abstained from voting. He explained his action thus: "I, as a servant of God, do not have the right to decide matters of life and death." Which, when you think about it, was also, in its way, a perfectly valid point.

Perhaps then we are guided by rational considerations? I have already submitted, however, that even if there were every logical reason to retain the death penalty, we would still be against it.

Moral imperatives, then? But if the moral argument against the death penalty is so compelling, why is it not apparent to those who would retain this form of punishment?

The principles of "natural rights" perhaps? True, the American Declaration of Independence cites the "right to life" among the most important of human rights. But it also cites the "right to freedom" and yet we still put people in prison. No one would dispute that in certain circumstances, some human rights may legitimately be restricted. It has even been established what these circumstances are, namely "the exercise of the natural rights of every man has no bounds other than those that ensure to the other members of society the enjoyment of these same rights" (Article 4 of the French Declaration of the Rights of Man and the Citizen, 1789). What can we say, moreover, to our opponents when they invoke this principle to justify imposing the death penalty for murder? A murderer is indeed guilty of depriving another person of life – does it not then follow that he should forfeit his own right to life? Our stock response, that is, the victim is already dead and executing the murderer is not going to bring him back, is fairly weak. After all, putting a criminal in prison is not going to bring the victim back either; it is merely punishing the murderer for a crime that has already been committed.

Perhaps in order to understand our real motivation, and that of our opponents, we need to look at history.

The death penalty is often described as a relic of our barbarian past. However, during the "barbarian" period proper, that is following the collapse of ancient civilisations and before the advent of the modern age, capital punishment was actually applied very rarely compared with the era of absolute monarchies and the following two centuries (except for the last thirty to forty years). During the "barbarian" or early feudal period in Europe, individuals were sentenced to death only if they made an attempt

on the life of the sovereign or tried to encroach upon the monarch's authority, or if they committed sacrilege, that is if they attempted to undermine the
religious institutions upheld by these same authorities, or, in modern jargon,
committed crimes against the state, which included ideological dissent. In
other words, the law, as upheld and implemented by these fledgling state
authorities, killed only those who, in its opinion, posed a threat to these
same authorities or their key institutions.

As far as other crimes were concerned, even murder tended to be punished
merely by a fine, payable to the victim's relatives. More common still was the
practice of blood feuds, governed by local custom. For example, from the
ninth to the eleventh century in Iceland, a landowner whose relative had
been murdered would, rather than turning to the law, round up the members of the household in order to hunt down and kill the perpetrator.
Perhaps, then, it is not so much the death penalty that should be regarded
as a relic of our barbarian past as mob law or vendettas, still practised in
some parts of the world today.

Everything changed with the emergence of powerful states, which effectively removed their subjects' right to revenge and appropriated it for themselves. In a parody, as it were, of the biblical expression "vengeance is mine,
I will repay", the state took on the role of God. Not just in the sphere of law
and order but in many other areas of social activity besides. In general, the
people of Europe accepted this revolutionary social development and blood
feuds became a punishable offence.

More recent European history, that is, the past two hundred years or so, has
seen yet another shift in the role of the state in society. The liberal and
democratic concepts that emerged in the eighteenth century treat state
authority as a public institution which, although extremely important for citizens, also poses a major threat to their freedom and thus needs to be kept
under constant public scrutiny. Not surprisingly, it was during this period,
when deification of the state and its attendant values was on the wane, that
certain thinkers (such as Beccaria and Kant) began to question the state's
right to dispose of human life.

Strictly speaking, the most erudite defenders of the death penalty could
legitimately argue that in a democratic, law-governed state, the right to execute people is vested not in the state itself but in the law – that is, the common will, as expressed through the language of law. Society has merely
reclaimed that which was once taken away from it.

Certainly, too, the notions of "common will", "the common weal" and
"virtue" as well as other such supra-personal concepts did at first seem to be

one of the cornerstones of the new social order, and a necessary substitute for the "divine right of kings", that is "legalised despotism". It took the tragic experience of the French Revolution (during which Maximilien Robespierre, one of the most vehement opponents of the death penalty, but also one of the most loyal disciples of Jean-Jacques Rousseau, instituted the Reign of Terror) to make us realise that any "absolute" abstraction that puts itself above the individual and his rights invariably degenerates into a form of legalised despotism.

Over the years, the idea of abolishing the death penalty has increasingly come to be seen as a natural, logical consequence of liberalism.

It is important to realise that, on an historical timescale, the new system of values emerged only very recently. For the last two centuries, we have been living in a transitional period and cannot yet be sure of our ultimate destination. For while in some western European countries and North America certain elements of this value system would appear to have already become part of the national culture, the same cannot be said, alas, of the rest of the world.

What exactly does "part of the national culture" mean? In my view, it can mean only one thing, namely that the values in question are shared by a significant part of the national élite – the intelligentsia, creative, artistic and even political circles. And, of course, by that section of the public that is inclined to listen to the opinions of the liberal intelligentsia. In the countries just mentioned, such people may, in some instances, already constitute the majority.

But there is also, of course, another section of society that is willing enough to accept the obvious benefits that come from living in a modern, caring, liberal, democratic state, but who are positively disinclined to accept the rather less obvious consequences of a liberal, democratic concept of society. In some ways, these people may be said to belong – consciously or, more likely subconsciously – to an earlier age. In their eyes, the abolition of state executions for crimes they instinctively feel deserve the death penalty appears as a kind of treachery. This sentiment, which is more in the nature of a primaeval instinct and almost impossible to put into words, may be summarised as follows: "We've been cheated – we handed over our right to take vengeance on murderers to the state, and now it's refusing to exercise that right".

Inevitably there are, and always will be, politicians who are prepared to exploit this instinct. I am willing to wager that, for the most part, these are the very same politicians who are inclined to question other more popular values of modern European civilisation as well. An extreme political expression of the denial of this civilisation can be seen in the totalitarian regimes of the twentieth century. It was no coincidence that these regimes extended the use of the death penalty to the extent that they did, including even in peacetime (the short-lived abolition of the death penalty in the USSR at the end of the 1940s merely serves to confirm my point – the Soviet authorities could not hold out for even three years without capital punishment). To the more traditional motives ascribed to supporters of the death penalty must be added the anxious reluctance of totalitarian states to relinquish even a modicum of power to the people. I sometimes think that the execution by firing squad of a million or so people in Russia between 1937 and 1939 was no more than an act of self-assertion by the Soviet regime, a case of "showing them who's boss". I simply cannot see any other rational explanation for the atrocities of the Stalinist era.

Even after the victory over nazi Germany and the collapse of communism, however, the totalitarian reflex continues to find support among the champions of so-called "national traditions", "state interests", "great powers" and "special paths of development". Thus, in the Russian Parliament, when it came to voting on the ratification of Protocol No. 6 to the European Convention on Human Rights, the communists, Zhirinovsky supporters, members of the agrarian party , and so on, all voted against.

Thus, arguments "for" and "against" the death penalty are almost worthless, since everything depends on how far the individuals concerned consider themselves staunch supporters or opponents of the liberal tradition. Surveys of public opinion show that even in countries with well-developed democracies, the majority of the population usually remains opposed to abolition. What, then, of countries that have set out on the path of democratic reform only fairly recently and still lack confidence in pursuing it?

The questions arising are: does our demand for rapid abolition of the death penalty not contradict the basic principles of democracy? Should we not win over public opinion first, and only then, having obtained public support, introduce the relevant changes in national legislation? Can democratic policies run counter to the will of the majority?

My profound conviction is that they can and they must.

It is not simply a matter of what this or that elector thinks about abolition *per se*. The issue is what he or she thinks about a specific system of values, of which demands for abolition are already an integral part. Incidentally, this point concerns not only the abolition of the death penalty, but also such anachronisms as obligatory military service, the gulf between the rights of citizens and non-citizens, severe restrictions on the right to immigrate and certain other legal institutions that enable the authorities to control human destinies. As it happens, the majority of a population is frequently in favour of archaic, cruel and anti-liberal solutions to these problems.

Fortunately, in democratically developed countries the same majority, whilst not approving a series of "progressive" liberal demands, consistently comes out in favour of freedom as a whole. Does this denote inconsistency on its part? Yes, but it is also reasonable: by entrusting the running of the country and the promulgation of laws to advocates of specific social values, electors are making a principled choice. Of course, it is the inescapable duty of an honest politician to explain to the electorate what stance he or she would take on important issues if elected, even if this stance is unpopular: for example, support for the abolition of capital punishment (thank heavens, in Europe this can now be expressed only as "against the restoration of the death penalty"). If the electors dislike these personal moral choices so much that they prefer to trust Le Pen or Zhirinovsky, then that is their right. This has long been the well-known paradox of democracy: freedom of choice implies the possibility to choose lack of freedom.

In any event, among the "package deals" offered as political programmes in present-day western Europe, including a set of approaches to solving current problems based on common fundamental principles, electors clearly prefer the package marked "freedom, democracy, human rights". They are even prepared to accept certain unpopular decisions, having already understood that these decisions are an integral part of the package.

Of course, this raises two problems.

The first is as follows: let us assume that a political figure appears, claiming to support freedom and democracy, but at the same time supporting the death penalty. He persuades the electorate that freedom and humanity are one thing, but that preserving the lives of criminals who have lost any human qualities is quite another. He might, for example, point to the expe-rience of the United States, a free and democratic society, where the num-ber of executions is nevertheless among the highest in the world.

Electors find it all the easier to believe him because, in their heart of hearts, they think in the same way. In the current intellectual outlook, will such a person not be at a distinct advantage over more appropriate rivals?

The second problem is this: what is to be done with the world surrounding western Europe, where the entire system of liberal values is continuously being called into question? Public opinion surveys in the Russian Federation on the question of the death penalty make the blood run cold. But how could they fail to shock, when the parliamentary election results are even more horrifying?

As a matter of fact, it is these very questions that the present publication addresses. It focuses on the experience of international agreements prohibiting or restricting the use of the death penalty.

In the first instance, this refers to Protocol No. 6 to the European Convention of Human Rights, currently the most consistent international law instrument of this type. To a certain extent, its adoption by the Council of Europe's Parliamentary Assembly in 1980 and the 1994 decision to make compliance with this text a mandatory condition for membership of the Council of Europe offer responses to both the above questions.

Indeed, let us suppose that a certain European political leader is convinced of the benefits of reintroducing the death penalty into national legislation and has succeeded in convincing his fellow citizens of this view. However, in order to persuade them to act, he must also convince them that this step is worth relinquishing membership of a highly prestigious and nationally advantageous European club: this will be considerably more difficult. The psychological effect of grasping the indissoluble legal link between being part of European civilisation and repudiating the death penalty means more in this situation than hundreds of educational leaflets (I am not at all suggesting that such leaflets are not necessary: of course, they are useful, and the more there are, the better).

Alternatively, one of the so-called "new democracies" submits an application for membership of the Council of Europe. In so doing, the political leaders and population of the country concerned know that they will be obliged to part, permanently and speedily, with certain cherished "national traditions". Again, no one is foisting membership of the Council on anyone else; if a country's license to carry out legal killing is more important to it than entry into this élite international association, the Council is entitled to reject efforts to become a member. Admittedly, not a single state seems so far to have forgone the opportunity to join the Council of Europe under these conditions. Not a single state has so far suggested to other states that they should form a new association, a kind of "killers' club", the honorary members of which would be China, Iran, Saudi Arabia and, sad to say, the United States, that long-standing democracy.

In general, I believe that the issue of the positions taken by the United States and Japan, described in a few of the articles in this collection, is extremely important. After all, these countries have been accorded observer status with the Council of Europe. From a political point of view, this is perhaps logical; nevertheless, the Council of Europe is not guided by political expediency, but by legal principles. Of course, legal co-operation with the United States is as essential for Europe as air; but how can full legal co-operation be established with a country to which extradition must be considered inadmissible in numerous serious cases? To what extent is the Americans' well-known con-servatism compatible with the status they have been accorded in the Council of Europe? This problem must be resolved.

Roberto Toscano's Chapter 7, "The United Nations and the abolition of the death penalty" is devoted to the attempt to solve the problem on an inter-national scale. This refers to the 1989 Additional Protocol to the 1966 Covenant on Civil and Political Rights, as well as the resolution adopted by the United Nations in 1997 following an Italian proposal. These are extreme-ly important initiatives, but I must admit that I am not very confident in their early success.

On the one hand, the United Nations is an international rather than a regional forum, and thus any documents adopted by it are of worldwide significance. It is sufficient to recall the key role of the United Nations Universal Declaration of Human Rights in advancing freedom throughout the world (including the USSR, which famously abstained from the 1948 vote). On the other hand, it is a forum for governments rather than nations. For dictatorships, widely represented at the UN, the declarations or optional texts adopted by the United Nations mean absolutely nothing.

In addition, Toscano recalls the charge of "cultural imperialism" levelled against the initiators of the 1997 resolution. This accusation is the favourite weapon of African and Asian dictators, and now of Russian, Ukrainian, Belarusian and other politicians in particular, whenever the international community tries to force them to live in a civilised manner. We are invited to regard cruel conditions of prison confinement, violations of human dignity, capital punishment and persecution for freedom of speech as "national tra-ditions" that the callous west is trying to correct on the basis of its own logic. The saddest thing of all is that many European intellectuals tend to agree with this position. In other words, something is considered an inadmissible violation of human rights in Austria or Denmark, but in the Republic of Togo, China or Ukraine the same matter is an integral part of the cultural heritage. What is this – intellectual and cultural humility before the diversity of human societies? That is how its supporters like to explain this point of view, but none of them has volunteered to spend time in a Togolese or Chinese prison in order to verify his or her opinion. I would suggest that this is simply a new variant of ordinary European arrogance, bordering on racism. Alas, this arrogance is characteristic of even the best representatives of the western European élite.

The merits and failings of a global approach are obvious. Indeed, its merits reside in its universal nature; a decision taken in an international forum can be said to be taken on behalf of all humanity. Unfortunately, its failings are a consequence of its merits: any dissenting country can announce that such a decision is an attack on its sovereignty and, given the current political disparateness of the international community, which still prevails even after the collapse of communism, the United Nations simply does not have any real means of enforcement. (I will not touch here on the question of whether or not it is wise to use force to oblige someone to behave in a civilised manner.)

I believe that the European path of voluntary acceptance of the obligation to live according to specific rules is ultimately more effective, albeit less striking. Returning to the problem of the death penalty, I should like to say that, in my view, the Council of Europe has actually accomplished more than could have been expected even a few years ago.

Many of the contributors to this publication have described the Europe of 1998 as a territory that is free from this form of punishment. Of course, I believe this is something of an exaggeration, particularly in view of the recent scandal regarding Ukraine, the regrettable events in Chechnya, for which the Russian Government is still *de jure* responsible, the Russian Parliament's reluctance to ratify Protocol No. 6, the recent statement by the Serbian Minister of Justice about the need to restore the death penalty (not to mention the monstrous current state of affairs in that country) and so on. Nevertheless, enormous progress has been made.

Of course, it is essential to advance further. We must strengthen the legal basis of the European abolition movement until the death penalty has been permanently abolished *de jure*, ensure constant monitoring of the situation, and carry out educational activities. And we should never, in any circumstances, relinquish what has already been achieved. Most importantly of all, on the issue of the abolition of the death penalty we must not accept the "double standards" of which Europe as a whole and the Council of Europe in particular are regularly guilty in other matters connected with human rights.

APPENDICES

APPENDICES

I. Protocol No. 6 to the Convention for the Protection of Human Rights and Fundamental Freedoms, concerning the Abolition of the Death Penalty (ETS No. 114)

Strasbourg, 28.IV.1983

The member States of the Council of Europe, signatory to this Protocol to the Convention for the Protection of Human Rights and Fundamental Freedoms, signed at Rome on 4 November 1950 (hereinafter referred to as "the Convention"),

Considering that the evolution that has occurred in several member States of the Council of Europe expresses a general tendency in favour of abolition of the death penalty;

Have agreed as follows:

Article 1 – Abolition of the death penalty

The death penalty shall be abolished. No one shall be condemned to such penalty or executed.

Article 2 – Death penalty in time of war

A State may make provision in its law for the death penalty in respect of acts committed in time of war or of imminent threat of war; such penalty shall be applied only in the instances laid down in the law and in accordance with its provisions. The State shall communicate to the Secretary General of the Council of Europe the relevant provisions of that law.

Article 3 – Prohibition of derogations

No derogation from the provisions of this Protocol shall be made under Article 15 of the Convention.

---

1. Headings of articles added and text amended according to the provisions of Protocol No. 11 (ETS No. 155) as from its entry into force on 1 November 1998.

Article 4 – Prohibition of reservations

No reservation may be made under Article 57 of the Convention in respect of the provisions of this Protocol.

Article 5 – Territorial application

1   Any State may at the time of signature or when depositing its instrument of ratification, acceptance or approval, specify the territory or territories to which this Protocol shall apply.

2   Any State may at any later date, by a declaration addressed to the Secretary General of the Council of Europe, extend the application of this Protocol to any other territory specified in the declaration. In respect of such territory the Protocol shall enter into force on the first day of the month following the date of receipt of such declaration by the Secretary General.

3   Any declaration made under the two preceding paragraphs may, in respect of any territory specified in such declaration, be withdrawn by a notification addressed to the Secretary General. The withdrawal shall become effective on the first day of the month following the date of receipt of such notification by the Secretary General.

Article 6 – Relationship to the Convention

As between the States Parties the provisions of Articles 1 to 5 of this Protocol shall be regarded as additional articles to the Convention and all the provisions of the Convention shall apply accordingly.

Article 7 – Signature and ratification

The Protocol shall be open for signature by the member States of the Council of Europe, signatories to the Convention. It shall be subject to ratification, acceptance or approval. A member State of the Council of Europe may not ratify, accept or approve this Protocol unless it has, simultaneously or previously, ratified the Convention. Instruments of ratification, acceptance or approval shall be deposited with the Secretary General of the Council of Europe.

Article 8 – Entry into force

1   This Protocol shall enter into force on the first day of the month following the date on which five member States of the Council of Europe have expressed their consent to be bound by the Protocol in accordance with the provisions of Article 7.

2 In respect of any member State which subsequently expresses its consent to be bound by it, the Protocol shall enter into force on the first day of the month following the date of the deposit of the instrument of ratification, acceptance or approval.

Article 9 – Depositary functions

The Secretary General of the Council of Europe shall notify the member States of the Council of:

a any signature;

b the deposit of any instrument of ratification, acceptance or approval;

c any date of entry into force of this Protocol in accordance with Articles 5 and 8;

d any other act, notification or communication relating to this Protocol.

In witness whereof the undersigned, being duly authorised thereto, have signed this Protocol.

Done at Strasbourg, this 28th day of April 1983, in English and in French, both texts being equally authentic, in a single copy which shall be deposited in the archives of the Council of Europe. The Secretary General of the Council of Europe shall transmit certified copies to each member State of the Council of Europe.

II. CHART OF SIGNATURES AND RATIFICATIONS OF THE EUROPEAN CONVENTION ON HUMAN RIGHTS BY MEMBER STATES OF THE COUNCIL OF EUROPE[1]

Member states	Date of signature	Date of ratification or accession	Date of entry into force	R: Reservations D: Declarations T: Territorial Declaration
Albania				
Andorra	22/01/96	22/01/96	01/02/96*	
Austria	28/04/83	05/01/84	01/03/85*	
Belgium	28/04/83	10/12/98	01/01/99	
Bulgaria				
Croatia	06/11/96	05/11/97	01/12/97*	
Cyprus				
Czech Republic	21/02/91[1]	18/03/92[2]	01/01/93*	
Denmark	28/04/83	01/12/83	01/03/85*	
Estonia	14/05/93	17/04/98	01/05/98*	
Finland	05/05/89	10/05/90	01/06/90*	
France	28/04/83	17/02/86	01/03/86*	
Germany	28/04/83	05/07/89	01/08/89*	D
Greece	02/05/83	08/09/98	01/10/98*	
Hungary	06/11/90	05/11/92	01/12/92*	
Iceland	24/04/85	22/05/87	01/06/87*	
Ireland	24/06/94	24/06/94	01/07/94*	
Italy	21/10/83	29/12/88	01/01/89*	
Latvia	26/06/98			
Liechtenstein	15/11/90	15/11/90	01/12/90*	
Lithuania	18/01/99			
Luxembourg	28/04/83	19/02/85	01/03/85*	
Malta	26/03/91	26/03/91	01/04/91*	
Moldova	02/05/96	12/09/97	01/10/97*	
Netherlands	28/04/83	25/04/86	01/05/86*	T
Norway	28/04/83	25/10/88	01/11/88*	
Poland				
Portugal	28/04/83	02/10/86	01/11/86*	
Romania	15/12/93	20/06/94	01/07/94*	
Russia	16/04/97			
San Marino	01/03/89	22/03/89	01/04/89*	
Slovakia	21/02/91[1]	18/03/92[2]	01/01/93*	
Slovenia	14/05/93	28/06/94	01/07/94*	

1. An updated list of signatures and ratifications of treaties by member states is reproduced in the Council of Europe's loose-leaf publication *Chart showing signatures and ratifications of conventions and agreements concluded within the Council of Europe*. It can also be obtained directly from the Treaty Office of the Council of Europe:
E-mail: treaty.office@coe.int – Fax +33 (0)3 88 41 37 38

Member states	Date of signature	Date of ratification or accession	Date of entry into force	R: Reservations D: Declarations T: Territorial Declaration
Spain	28/04/83	14/01/85	01/03/85*	
Sweden	28/04/83	09/02/84	01/03/85*	
Switzerland	28/04/83	13/10/87	01/11/87*	
"The former Yugoslav Republic of Macedonia"	14/06/96	10/04/97	01/05/97*	
Turkey				
Ukraine	05/05/97			
United Kingdom	27/01/99			

* State having made declarations pursuant to Articles 25 and 46 (see following chart)
1 Date of signature by the Czech and Slovak Federal Republic
2 Date of deposit of the instrument of ratification of the Czech and Slovak Federal Republic

III. EUROPE: A DEATH PENALTY-FREE CONTINENT

Report by the Committee on Legal Affairs and Human Rights
Rapporteur: Mrs Renate Wohlwend, Liechtenstein, Group of the European People's Party (Doc. 8340 – 8 April 1999)

Summary

The new millennium will mark the fiftieth anniversary of the European Convention on Human Rights and the Council of Europe member states should celebrate this event as a death penalty-free continent. In recent years the impetus towards abolition has become stronger and stronger, with many member states ratifying Protocol No. 6 or abolishing the death penalty in their domestic law. It is a very positive sign that an overwhelming majority of new member states, notwithstanding the difficulties inherent in their economic and political transition, have abolished the death penalty. Nonetheless, one cannot ignore the news received from some countries, which shows that the Council of Europe must continue to strive for the most fundamental right of all.

I. Draft resolution

1.   The Assembly, referring to its Resolutions 1044 (1994) and 1097 (1996), reaffirms its belief that the application of the death penalty constitutes inhuman and degrading punishment and a violation of the most fundamental human right, that to life itself. It reiterates its firm conviction that capital punishment, therefore, has no place in civilised, democratic societies governed by the rule of law.

2.   The Assembly is heartened by the fact that the number of executions in Council of Europe member states is steadily diminishing – from 18 in 1997 (of which 13 took place in Ukraine and 5 in the Russian Federation (Chechnya)) to a single one in 1998 (in the Russian Federation (Chechnya)).

3.   The Assembly is similarly encouraged by recent positive developments in several member states. It is pleased that, following ratification by Belgium and Greece, thirty member states have ratified Protocol No. 6. Also, since the signature of Protocol No. 6 by the United Kingdom and Lithuania, only five member states are not signatories of the Protocol, namely, Albania, Bulgaria, Cyprus, Poland and Turkey. Further, it congratulates Bulgaria, Cyprus, Estonia, Lithuania, Poland, as well as Georgia (applicant state) on their total

abolition in domestic law of the death penalty and it regrets that five member states – Albania, Latvia, the Russian Federation, Turkey and Ukraine – still retain the death penalty on their statute books.

4. However, the Assembly is concerned, that four member states, namely Albania, the Russian Federation, Latvia and Ukraine, still maintain prisoners on death row in violation of their commitment to abolish the death penalty within a certain period following accession to the Council of Europe.

5. Especially, the Assembly condemns in the strongest possible terms the executions that have taken place in Chechnya as a consequence of a fundamentalist interpretation of the Sharia. It calls on the responsible authorities to fully respect the moratorium on executions instituted by the Russian Federation.

6. These member states must realise that the Assembly is unwilling to reconsider their commitments with regard to the abolition of the death penalty. On the contrary, the Assembly will use all means at its disposal to ensure that commitments freely entered into are honoured.

7. It thus asks Albania, Latvia, the Russian Federation and Ukraine that they ratify Protocol No. 6 to the European Convention on Human Rights, to under no circumstances whatsoever carry out an execution, and to commute the sentence of all those condemned to death as soon as the death penalty is abolished. It acknowledges the efforts of the members of the Latvian Parliament in this respect and urges them to pursue total abolition.

8. Moreover, it urges all member states of the Council of Europe which have not yet done so, to sign and/or ratify Protocol No. 6 to the European Convention on Human Rights, in order that Europe may enter the third millennium as an execution – and death penalty – free zone.

9. Finally the Assembly decides – and calls on the whole of the Council of Europe, including the Committee of Ministers to do likewise – to offer full assistance to member states experiencing difficulties in abolishing the death penalty in particular by disseminating information and by organising awareness-raising seminars aimed at assuring support from governmental and from non-governmental circles.

II. Explanatory memorandum by Mrs Wohlwend

A. Introduction

1. In 1997, executions in the member states of the Council of Europe came to an alarming total of 18 (Ukraine: 13; Chechnya: 5). In 1998, however, the situation improved and Europe became a practically execution-free zone,

tarnished only by events in Chechnya, where there was one execution in June 1998. In 1998 and early 1999 there have been two trends among the member states.

2.   First, there has been a consolidation of the legal basis for abolition as national legislation has been adopted abolishing the death penalty. Poland, Bulgaria and Lithuania have done away with the death penalty and Latvia has begun the legislative process necessary to do so. In addition, some long-standing member states have decided to sign or ratify Protocol No. 6 to the European Convention on Human Rights and hence to enshrine abolition in domestic law. Greece and Belgium have ratified the Protocol and the United Kingdom is about to do so. These states should be warmly congratulated and those states which have recently embraced abolition should be encouraged to consolidate their achievements by ratifying Protocol No. 6.

3.   To date, thirty of the Council of Europe's forty member states have ratified Protocol No. 6: Andorra (1996), Austria (1984), Belgium (1998), Croatia (1997), the Czech Republic (1993), Denmark (1985), Estonia (1998), Finland (1990), France (1986), Germany (1989), Greece (1998), Hungary (1992), Iceland (1987), Ireland (1994), Italy (1989), Liechtenstein (1990), Luxembourg (1985), Malta (1991), Moldova (1997), the Netherlands (1986), Norway (1988), Portugal (1986), Romania (1994), San Marino (1989), Slovakia (1993), Slovenia (1994), Spain (1985), Sweden (1985), Switzerland (1987), and "the former Yugoslav Republic of Macedonia" (1997). Five other member states have signed Protocol No. 6 but have not yet deposited their instruments of ratification: Latvia, Lithuania, Russia, Ukraine and the United Kingdom. Bulgaria and Poland have abolished the death penalty under domestic law but have not yet signed Protocol No. 6. Only Albania and Turkey have yet to abolish the death penalty in domestic law or sign Protocol No. 6.

4.   These advances should not obscure the concern aroused by certain central and eastern European countries attempting to curb an increase in the crime rate by calling into question their commitments vis-à-vis the Council of Europe. Certain members of the Albanian, Russian and Ukraine governments regularly use this argument to justify the possibility of lifting the moratorium. The main aim of any such gesture would be to assuage the demands of the public, most of whom are opposed to abolition.

5.   Apart from the fact that it is linked to one-off events – a serial killer in Ukraine, a political assassination in Russia, a murder of police officers in Albania – this argument does not hold water in any non-populist crime policy. It should be recalled that there is no scientifically proven correlation between the death penalty and a lower crime rate. In fact, it could be argued

that by institutionalising death, we create a more violent society, the prime example being the United States.

6.   Once again I would like to denounce the argument which the Russian authorities alone put forward, namely that the abolition of the death penalty is impossible because of the cost of keeping the convicts in prison. Not only is this argument contemptible because it connects human life to budgetary considerations, but it is also fallacious. Although it is estimated that there are some 1 000 prisoners under sentence of death in Russia, this is a derisory figure in terms of the cost, compared with the total Russian prison population of 1 200 000.

7.   In any event, the authorities of the member states in question – Albania, Russia and Ukraine – must realise that the Assembly totally rules out any possibility of releasing them from their commitment to abolish the death penalty. As early as 1994, the Assembly formally acknowledged that the death penalty constituted inhuman and degrading punishment in itself and a violation of the most fundamental human right, namely that to life. The Assembly has consistently warned member states which are reluctant to honour their commitments to bring an end to all executions and abolish the death penalty "that it will take all necessary steps to ensure compliance with commitments entered into" (Resolution 1112 (1997)) – most recently this was the case with Ukraine, at the January 1999 part-session. Since 1994 the Assembly has made it a prerequisite for all states wishing to join the Council of Europe to commit themselves to ratifying Protocol No. 6 within three years of accession and introducing a moratorium on executions in the meantime.

B. Developments since the report submitted to the Assembly in June 1996 (Document 7589)

8.   The developments described below are based on information provided by the authorities of the states concerned and non-governmental organisations, or were gleaned from the press and any other available source. Wherever possible I have cross-checked our sources but the instability and the impenetrability of the political situation in certain areas has made it impossible to put forward figures with any degree of certainty.

9.   Only states in which there were developments with regard to the abolition of the death penalty during 1997 and 1998 are cited. Also, this report will not consider the situation in states with observer status with the Council of Europe in which the death penalty still applies – Japan and the United States – since this is shortly to be covered in detail in a separate report. For a more complete presentation of the arguments in favour of abolition, you

are invited to consult Mr Franck's excellent explanatory memorandum on the subject (Document 7154) and my report of 1996 (Document 7589).

i. Council of Europe member states

Albania

10. Albania has been a member of the Council of Europe since July 1995 but it has not yet abolished the death penalty, which still applies to seven different offences. Nonetheless, Albania has applied a moratorium on executions since 29 June 1995, introduced with a view to its accession to the Council of Europe. Given the commitments entered into by Albania on joining the Council, it should have signed Protocol No. 6 by 13 July 1998.

11. As far as I know, no executions have taken place since the introduction of the moratorium. However, the Albanian courts continue to sentence people to death. On 16 December 1998, the Supreme Court of Tirana sentenced four people to death. This sentence follows on from another passed on 23 October 1997.

12. The violent events of late 1997 and a substantial rise in the crime rate have led certain Albanian political leaders, apparently supported by the majority of the public, to suggest that the moratorium should be lifted. This situation has prompted both the Secretary General of the Council of Europe and the Bureau of the Assembly to remind the Albanian Government of its commitments as a member state.

Belgium

13. Under a law of 1 August 1996 the death penalty was totally abolished. There had been no executions since 1950. Belgium signed Protocol No. 6 in 1983 and ratified it on December 1998. It entered into force in Belgium on 1 January 1999. Belgium has also ratified the Second Optional Protocol to the International Covenant on Civil and Political Rights, designed to abolish the death penalty worldwide.

Bulgaria

14. On 10 December 1998, by an overwhelming majority, the Bulgarian Parliament passed a law abolishing the death penalty for all crimes. The penalty was applicable to the perpetrators of high treason, espionage, assassination, war crimes and genocide. Until then the courts had continued to pass death sentences but they were not carried out because of a moratorium introduced by the parliament on 20 July 1990. The last execution took

place on 4 November 1989. The death penalty has been replaced by a non-commutable sentence of life imprisonment not applicable to persons under 20 years of age and women who are pregnant at the time of the offence or the judgment.

15. In accordance with his commitments, the Bulgarian Vice-President has commuted the twenty-one death sentences passed between 1990 and 1998 to life imprisonment.

16. Bulgaria has not yet signed and ratified Protocol No. 6. This state of affairs should be seen in parallel with the statements of politicians and prison governors in favour of the death penalty. These statements simply reflect the opinion of the public, 52% of whom are in favour of the death penalty for particularly cruel murders, according to a poll carried out by the MBMD agency in Sofia. However, there is reason to hope that the abolition of the death penalty will be followed by the signature and ratification of Protocol No. 6.

Cyprus

17. On 18 February 1999 the House of Representatives unanimously voted for the abolition of the death penalty under domestic law. The death penalty was retained only for certain military offences. The government immediately proceeded to complete the necessary legislative modifications so as to enable the signing of Protocol No. 6; its ratification will take place at the earliest possible moment.

Croatia

18. The death penalty has been abolished for all crimes. Croatia has signed and ratified Protocol No. 6, which came into force in Croatia on 1 December 1997.

Estonia

19. Estonia signed Protocol No. 6 on accession to the Council of Europe in May 1993. The last execution took place in September 1991. In December 1996 the Estonian Parliament adopted an amendment to the criminal code introducing life imprisonment as an alternative to the death sentence. This reform enabled the parliament to vote in favour of ratification of Protocol No. 6, which was carried out on 17 April 1998, thereby entirely abolishing the death penalty in peacetime. The sentences of the eight prisoners on death row were commuted to life imprisonment.

Greece

20. Greece totally abolished the death penalty in 1993. This enabled it to deposit the instrument for the ratification of Protocol No. 6 on 8 September 1998 and bring it into force in Greece on 1 October 1998.

21. On 5 May 1997, Greece signed the Second Optional Protocol to the International Covenant on Civil and Political Rights, designed to abolish the death penalty worldwide.

Latvia

22. In September 1996 the Latvian President, Guntis Ulmanis, notified the Parliamentary Assembly of the Council of Europe that an informal moratorium had been introduced by means of the systematic granting of a presidential pardon. As in other member states where a *de jure* moratorium has not been introduced, the Latvian courts have continued to hand down death sentences. Since the introduction of the moratorium, the Latvian courts have handed down seven death sentences, including five in 1998. Latvia signed Protocol No. 6 on 26 June 1998.

23. In May 1998, the Latvian Parliament, the Saeima, rejected a bill aimed at removing the death penalty from Latvian law. The lack of *de jure* abolition and the attitude of the Saeima prompted Leni Fischer, who was then the President of the Parliamentary Assembly, and the Secretary General of the Council of Europe to approach the Latvian authorities on the matter.

24. This approach bore fruit on 6 January 1999, when the Human Rights Committee of the Latvian Parliament adopted a bill on the ratification of Protocol No. 6. The bill was passed on its first reading on 4 February 1999 by an extremely large majority. The ultimate adoption of this bill will entail an amendment to the criminal code, abolishing the death penalty. According to my sources, the final text provides for life imprisonment. A fixed term of imprisonment is not being considered because public opinion is hostile to this idea.

Liechtenstein

25. The death penalty was abolished for all crimes on 1 January 1989. On 10 December 1998, Liechtenstein signed the Second Optional Protocol to the International Covenant on Civil and Political Rights, designed to abolish the death penalty worldwide.

Lithuania

26. Lithuania has been a member of the Council of Europe since 1993 and there have been no executions in the country since 1995. On 9 December 1998 the Lithuanian Constitutional Court held that the provisions of the criminal code on the death penalty were unconstitutional. On 22 December 1998 the Lithuanian Parliament passed a law amending several provisions of the criminal code and confirming the abolition of the death penalty. At the same time another law was passed reducing death sentences already passed to life imprisonment. Nine prisoners were thought to be on death row at the time. Adding the final touch to these changes, Lithuania signed Protocol No. 6 on 18 January 1999.

Moldova

28. Moldova abolished the death penalty in December 1995 and signed Protocol No. 6 in May 1996. It was ratified in September 1997 and entered into force on 1 October 1997.

Poland

29. The Polish Parliament permanently abolished the death penalty when the Diet adopted a new criminal code on 6 June 1997. The new code came into force on 1 January 1998. There have been no executions since 1988.

30. The new code provides for sentences of life imprisonment. Courts of first instance may add a condition to these sentences making it impossible for prisoners to request release on parole. In this event, prisoners may request a remission of sentence from the judge responsible for the execution of sentences once they have served twenty-five years of their sentence.

31. Poland has not yet signed or ratified Protocol No. 6.

Russian Federation

32. The death penalty is still on the statute books in force in the Russian Federation. The new criminal code which came into force on 1 January 1997 substantially reduced the number of offences incurring the death penalty. This positive development should not be allowed to conceal the fact that the five offences which remain out of the twenty-eight are those which account for the vast majority of death sentences.

33. In keeping with its commitments, the Russian Federation has been applying a moratorium on executions. The last execution took place on

2 August 1996. Though the situation is still very confused, there does seem to be a trend towards abolition in the medium term.

34. The Russian Federation has also signed Protocol No. 6 but omitted to deposit its instrument of ratification by 28 February 1999, thus failing to honour one of its commitments to the Council of Europe.

35. Figures for the number of prisoners on death row vary according to sources. Anatoly Pristavkin, the Chair of the Presidential Pardons Commission, informed the Committee in January 1999 that he estimated the number of prisoners on death row at 620. The Minister of Justice gives a figure of 839 prisoners. It should be noted that Mr Pristavkin bases his figures on final sentences, the only ones against which it is possible to lodge an appeal with the Pardons Commission.

36. In response to various political assassinations, particularly that of the Liberal member of parliament Galina Starovoitova, December 1998 was punctuated by numerous contradictory statements from Russian governmental and political circles. The Prime Minister, Yevgeny Primakov, made a particularly egregious statement in which he proposed the physical elimination of those who undermined society. Comments of this kind can only be condemned, particularly when they come from members of the government. It is worth noting that the Orthodox Church, in the person of the Patriarch of all the Russians, Alexy II, has come out in favour of abolition.

37. These statements seem to be aimed primarily at the Russian electorate. In response to the Council of Europe's enquiries, the Russian Government said that policies to combat crime would respect human rights and honour Russia's international undertakings, particularly those given to the Council of Europe.

38. This attitude has been borne out by a particularly welcome development at the beginning of this year, in the form of the Russian Constitutional Court's decision on 2 February 1999 to suspend all death sentences until a law is passed setting up assize courts with a jury for all capital cases.

39. This initiative goes hand in hand with that of the Minister of Justice, Pavel Krasheninikov, who has presented the government with a bill on the abolition of the death penalty which would enable Russia to ratify Protocol No. 6. The bill abolishes capital punishment and replaces it with life imprisonment or imprisonment for twenty-five years. The courts would be required to commute every death sentence they have already passed to one of these two sentences.

40. Likewise, in January 1999, Anatoly Pristavkin, the Chair of the Presidential Pardons Commission, told the Parliamentary Assembly Committee on Legal Affairs and Human Rights that he hoped that all the death sentences delivered in the past would be commuted to prison sentences by the summer of 1999. This policy represents a U-turn because until recently the Pardons Commission was no longer forwarding the appeals it received to the President. Russian criminal law prohibits all executions before the President has given his opinion. This wait-and-see approach was prompted by the hope that a *de jure* moratorium would soon be introduced.

41. These highly positive developments, which are largely the result of the Council of Europe's efforts, should not be allowed to obscure concern about the lawless areas which still exist on Russian territory, particularly in Chechnya.

42. Chechnya applies the death penalty in spite of Russian law and Russia's international undertakings. Executions are often carried out in public and civilians are allowed to take part in the killing, particularly members of the family of the criminal's victim. According to Amnesty International, five people were executed in 1997. According to the same source, another execution took place in June 1998 and thirty people or more are on death row. However, in complete contradiction to this, the representative of the Chechen Republic to the Russian Federation told Amnesty International, in May 1998, that the Chechen authorities were applying a moratorium on executions. Unfortunately this undertaking seems merely a pious hope in view of the radicalisation of the Chechen leadership, which is reacting to an extremely depressed economic situation by attempting to pursue a repressive policy based on a fundamentalist interpretation of the Islamic Sharia law.

Slovakia

43. On 22 September 1998, Slovakia, which had already ratified Protocol No. 6 in 1993, signed the Second Optional Protocol to the International Covenant on Civil and Political Rights, designed to abolish the death penalty worldwide.

"The former Yugoslav Republic of Macedonia"

44. "The former Yugoslav Republic of Macedonia" abolished the death penalty in its 1991 Constitution and signed Protocol No. 6 in 1996. It was ratified in April 1997 and entered into force on 1 May 1997.

Turkey

45. The death penalty is still on the statute books in Turkey, which, although it is a member state, has not yet signed Protocol No. 6. However, it has applied a *de facto* moratorium since 1984. A bill to reform the criminal code is currently being examined by the Justice Committee of the Turkish Grand National Assembly. This bill, which comprises 522 sections, proposes far-reaching reforms to Turkish criminal law, abolishing the death penalty during peacetime.

Ukraine

46. According to the information at my disposal, Ukraine carried out thirteen executions in 1997. A letter signed by Ms Stanik, Minister of Justice, and sent to the President of the Assembly on 31 March 1998, states that Ukraine carried out 212 executions between November 1995, when it joined the Council of Europe, and 11 March 1997, the date of the most recent execution. It would seem that there were no executions in 1998 though there are doubts about the period from 11 March to 31 December 1997. As the death penalty has not been abolished by law, 146 people were sentenced to death in 1998, according to the President of Ukraine's Supreme Court. According to Amnesty International, there were 345 people on death row in Ukraine in November 1998. Ukraine signed Protocol No. 6 on 5 May 1997.

47. A *de facto* moratorium has been introduced by President Leonid Kuchma, who refuses to consider any of the appeals for pardon sent to him, thereby preventing any of the sentences from being implemented.

48. In September 1998 a bill on the abolition of the death penalty was given a first reading in the Ukraine Parliament. Furthermore, the Ukraine presidency has said that the parliament must adopt a *de jure* moratorium by July 1999. These initiatives seem to have been elicited by the strong reactions of the Parliamentary Assembly of the Council of Europe in December 1998 and January 1999. If they succeed, Ukraine will have met all of the conditions set by the Assembly in Resolution 1145 (1998).

49. As well as calling for an end to executions, the Assembly asked Ukraine to dispel the secrecy surrounding executions and those awaiting execution, which entailed major risks of human rights violations. According to statements made by Ms S. Stanik, the Ukrainian Minister of Justice, to the Secretary General of the Council of Europe, the only information which will be kept secret from now on is the name of the executioner, the place of execution and details of how the execution will be carried out.

Once again the Ukrainian authorities must be urged to honour the commitments they entered into when joining the Council of Europe and to look to the future by overcoming party political divides and overriding a public opinion apparently in favour of the death penalty.

United Kingdom

50. The United Kingdom abolished the death penalty for murder in 1965 and the last execution took place in 1964. However, various laws still provided for the death penalty in cases of treason, acts of piracy involving violence and offences specific to military law.

51. On 20 May 1998, during the parliamentary debate on the adoption of the 1998 Human Rights Act, incorporating the Convention for the Protection of Human Rights and Fundamental Freedoms into domestic law, the House of Commons voted in favour of incorporating Protocol No. 6. As a result, the Criminal Justice Act was amended to remove the death penalty for treason and piracy. The last offences in military law incurring the death sentence will be amended accordingly as part of the five-yearly review of the Armed Forces Act in 2001.

52. These changes enabled the United Kingdom to sign Protocol No. 6 on 27 January 1998.

ii. Applicant countries

Armenia

53. Faced with a public opinion largely in favour of the death penalty, Armenian political leaders have not yet come out in favour of the abolition of the death penalty. There are currently twenty-eight people awaiting execution in Armenia. A bill to abolish the death penalty is still before parliament, having been given its first reading.

Azerbaijan

54. Azerbaijan has applied a moratorium on the death penalty since 1993. Following a proposal by President Aliev in January 1998, the Azerbaijani Parliament voted for the abolition of the death penalty on 10 February 1998. The sentences of the 128 prisoners on death row were commuted.

Bosnia and Herzegovina

55. The Bosnian Parliament has had special guest status with the Council of Europe since January 1994. Bosnia and Herzegovina submitted a formal

application for membership in July 1995. The peace agreement of 1995 known as the "Dayton Agreement" contains a formal undertaking to abolish the death penalty. The Supreme Court of the Republika Srpska has decided that the execution of a death sentence is contrary to international human rights principles. Similarly, the Human Rights Chamber of the Federation has stated that the execution of any death penalty would be contrary to Protocol No. 6 and has asked the authorities to ensure that no executions can be carried out. In July 1998, the Federation adopted a new criminal code abolishing the death penalty. Because this code has not yet been published in the official journal of the Federation, it has not yet entered into force. However, as the eminent lawyers state in their report on Bosnia and Herzegovina "it is [...] safe to say that the death penalty is not applied in Bosnia and Herzegovina" (As/Bur/BiH (1999) 1 rev.).

56. Furthermore, one must welcome the fact that the statute of the International Criminal Tribunal for the Former Yugoslavia adopted in May 1993 makes no provision for the death penalty even for the gravest human rights violations.

Belarus

57. In January 1997, the Parliamentary Assembly of the Council of Europe suspended the Belarus Parliament's special guest status following the constitutional changes introduced by President Lukashenko. The death penalty is still in force.

Georgia

58. The death penalty was abolished when the parliament adopted a new criminal code on 11 November 1997. In July 1997, as he is empowered to do, President Shevardnadze had commuted the fifty-four outstanding death sentences to twenty-year prison sentences.

59. Following the favourable Opinion issued by the Assembly in January 1999, Georgia's accession to the Council of Europe should be followed by the signature and ratification of Protocol No. 6. Six years ago Georgia introduced a moratorium, which it subsequently lifted for a while then re-introduced in February 1995. This about-turn was linked to the situation in the conflict zones of South Ossetia and Abkhazia. The ratification of Protocol No. 6 would confirm Georgia's intention not to reconsider abolition and forms part of the commitments detailed in the Opinion of the Assembly on accession to the Council of Europe (No. 209 (1999) paragraph 10.i.b).

Monaco

60. Article 20 of the Constitution of the Principality of Monaco of 17 December 1962 states that "the death penalty is abolished".

C. Conclusions

61. Recent developments are encouraging, but the debates they have triggered or are still eliciting in the member states prove that a step backwards may sometimes remain possible. For that reason, those states that have not yet done so should ratify Protocol No. 6 without reservation, thereby rendering abolition more lasting.

62. States which retain the death penalty for obsolete offences or crimes committed in wartime are similarly urged to abolish the death penalty entirely. Measures of this kind would set an example for countries which have begun the process of abolition.

63. The Assembly for its part must continue to defend its principles on the abolition of the death penalty to ensure that we can at last create a Europe entirely free of capital punishment. In five years, the Council of Europe has almost succeeded in making Europe an execution-free continent, the exception being one execution in Chechnya last year. These results are encouraging but they are not enough. The Assembly must continue its efforts. The Chechen authorities in particular must be warned that they will receive no assistance if the moratorium in force in the Russian Federation is not immediately and scrupulously applied. In addition, member states which are reluctant to honour their commitments should be urged to comply and, if necessary, be subjected to the sanctions which the Assembly proposes in Opinion No. 208 (1999), paragraph 18.iii.b.

64. In addition, the Assembly, and the entire Council of Europe, must offer their assistance to member states faced with obstacles in their efforts to abolish the death penalty, in particular by disseminating information on the subject and by organising awareness-raising seminars aimed at the governmental and non-governmental circles concerned. My most fervent hope is that these efforts will be successful and that Europe will enter the new millennium a death penalty-free continent.

Reference to committee: Resolutions 1097 (1996), 1111 (1997), 1112 (1997), 1145 (1998) and Order No. 538 (1998)

Draft resolution adopted by the committee on 1 March 1999 with 18 votes in favour, 3 votes against and 4 abstentions

SUGGESTED FURTHER READING

C. Boulanger (ed.) et al., *Zur Aktualität der Todesstrafe: Interdisziplinäre Beiträge gegen eine unmenschliche, grausame und ernierdrigende Strafe*, Berlin Verlag A. Spitz, Berlin, 1997.

R. Cario (ed.), *La peine de mort au seuil du troisième millénaire: hommage au professeur Antonio Beristain*, ERES, Toulouse, 1993.

M. Costanzo, *Just Revenge: Costs and Consequences of the Death Penalty*, Ph.D. thesis, St Martin Press, 1997.

H.A. Bedau, *The Death Penalty in America: current controversies*, Oxford University Press, Oxford, 1998.

J. Georcki, *Capital punishment, criminal law and social evolution*, Columbia University Press, New York, 1983.

S. Gross and R. Mauro, *Death and discrimination: racial disparities in capital sentencing*, Northeastern, Boston, 1989.

P. Hodgkinson, A. Rutherford (ed.), *Capital punishment: global issues and prospects*, Waterside, Winchester 1996.

R. Hood, *The Death Penalty: A Worldwide Perspective*. Second revised and up-dated edition, Oxford: Oxford University Press, 1996.

R. Hood, *The Death Penalty: A Worldwide Perspective: a report to the United Nations Committee on Crime Prevention and Control*, Clarendon Press, Oxford, 1991.

R. Hood, "The death penalty: the USA in a world perspective" *Florida State University Journal of Transnational Law and Policy*, Volume 6, Number 2, 1997, pp. 517-41.

R. Hood, "Capital punishment" in Michael Tonry (ed.), *The Handbook of Crime and Punishment*. Oxford University Press, New York, 1998, pp. 739-76.

J. Imbert, *La peine de mort*, PUF, Paris, 1993.

J. Megivern, *The Death Penalty: an historical and theological survey*, Paulist Press, Lancaster, 1997.

B.G. Ramcharan (ed.), *The right to life in international law*, Nijhoff, Lancaster, 1985.

W.A. Schabas, *The death penalty as cruel treatment and torture: capital punishment challenged in the world's courts*, Northeastern University Press, Boston, 1996.

W.A. Schabas, *The abolition of the death penalty in international law*, (2nd edn) 1997, Cambridge University Press, Cambridge.

V. Streib, *Death penalty and juveniles*, Indiana University Press, Indianapolis, 1987.

Sales agents for publications of the Council of Europe
Agents de vente des publications du Conseil de l'Europe

AUSTRALIA/AUSTRALIE
Hunter Publications, 58A, Gipps Street
AUS-3066 COLLINGWOOD, Victoria
Fax: (61) 33 9 419 7154
E-mail: Robd@mentis.com.au

AUSTRIA/AUTRICHE
Gerold und Co., Graben 31
A-1011 WIEN 1
Fax: (43) 1512 47 31 29
E-mail: buch@gerold.telecom.at

BELGIUM/BELGIQUE
La Librairie européenne SA
50, avenue A. Jonnart
B-1200 BRUXELLES 20
Fax: (32) 27 35 08 60
E-mail: info@libeurop.be

Jean de Lannoy
202, avenue du Roi
B-1060 BRUXELLES
Fax: (32) 25 38 08 41
E-mail: jean.de.lannoy@euronet.be

CANADA
Renouf Publishing Company Limited
5369 Chemin Canotek Road
CDN-OTTAWA, Ontario, K1J 9J3
Fax: (1) 613 745 76 60

CZECH REPUBLIC/RÉPUBLIQUE TCHÈQUE
USIS, Publication Service
Havelkova 22
CZ-130 00 Praha 3
Fax: (420) 2 242 21 484

DENMARK/DANEMARK
Munksgaard
Østergade 26A – Postbox 173
DK-1005 KØBENHAVN K
Fax: (45) 77 33 33 77
E-mail: direct@munksgaarddirect.dk

FINLAND/FINLANDE
Akateeminen Kirjakauppa
Keskuskatu 1, PO Box 218
FIN-00381 HELSINKI
Fax: (358) 9 121 44 50
E-mail: akatilaus@stockmann.fi

FRANCE
C.I.D.
131 boulevard Saint-Michel
F-75005 Paris
Fax: (33) 01 43 54 80 73
E-mail: lecarrer@msh-paris.fr

GERMANY/ALLEMAGNE
UNO Verlag
Proppelsdorfer Allee 55
D-53115 BONN
Fax: (49) 228 21 74 92
E-mail: unoverlag@aol.com

GREECE/GRÈCE
Librairie Kauffmann
Mavrokordatou 9
GR-ATHINAI 106 78
Fax: (30) 13 23 03 20

HUNGARY/HONGRIE
Euro Info Service/Magyarország
Margitsziget (Európa Ház),
H-1138 BUDAPEST
Fax: (361) 302 50 35
E-mail: euroinfo@mail.matav.hu

IRELAND/IRLANDE
Government Stationery Office
4-5 Harcourt Road
IRL-DUBLIN 2
Fax: (353) 14 75 27 60

ISRAEL/ISRAËL
ROY International
41 Mishmar Hayarden Street
PO Box 13056
IL-69865 TEL AVIV
Fax: (972) 3 648 60 39
E-mail: royil@netvision.net.il

ITALY/ITALIE
Libreria Commissionaria Sansoni
Via Duca di Calabria 1/1, CP 552
I-50125 FIRENZE
Fax: (39) 0 55 64 12 57
E-mail: licosa@ftbcc.it

MALTA/MALTE
L. Sapienza & Sons Ltd
26 Republic Street, PO Box 36
VALLETTA CMR 01
Fax: (356) 233 621

NETHERLANDS/PAYS-BAS
De Lindeboom Internationale Publikaties
PO Box 202
NL-7480 AE HAAKSBERGEN
Fax: (31) 53 572 92 96
E-mail: lindeboo@worldonline.nl

NORWAY/NORVÈGE
Akademika, A/S Universitetsbokhandel
PO Box 84, Blindern
N-0314 OSLO
Fax: (47) 22 85 30 53

POLAND/POLOGNE
Głowna Księgarnia Naukowa im. B. Prusa
Krakowskie Przedmiescie 7
PL-00-068 WARSZAWA
Fax: (48) 22 26 64 49

PORTUGAL
Livraria Portugal
Rua do Carmo, 70
P-1200 LISBOA
Fax: (351) 13 47 02 64

SPAIN/ESPAGNE
Mundi-Prensa Libros SA
Castelló 37
E-28001 MADRID
Fax: (34) 915 75 39 98
E-mail: libreria@mundiprensa.es

SWITZERLAND/SUISSE
Buchhandlung Heinimann & Co.
Kirchgasse 17
CH-8001 ZÜRICH
Fax: (41) 12 51 14 81

BERSY
Route d'Uvrier 15
CH-1958 LIVRIER/SION
Fax: (41) 27 203 73 32

UNITED KINGDOM/ROYAUME-UNI
TSO (formerly HMSO)
51 Nine Elms Lane
GB-LONDON SW8 5DR
Fax: (44) 171 873 82 00
E-mail: denise.perkins@theso.co.uk

**UNITED STATES and CANADA/
ÉTATS-UNIS et CANADA**
Manhattan Publishing Company
468 Albany Post Road, PO Box 850
CROTON-ON-HUDSON, NY 10520, USA
Fax: (1) 914 271 58 56
E-mail: Info@manhattanpublishing.com

STRASBOURG
Librairie Kléber
Palais de l'Europe
F-67075 STRASBOURG Cedex
Fax: +33 (0)3 88 52 91 21

Council of Europe Publishing/Editions du Conseil de l'Europe
F-67075 Strasbourg Cedex
Tel. +33 (0)3 88 41 25 81 – Fax +33 (0)3 88 41 39 10
E-mail: publishing@coe.fr – Website: http://book.coe.fr